Training
in the
Human Services

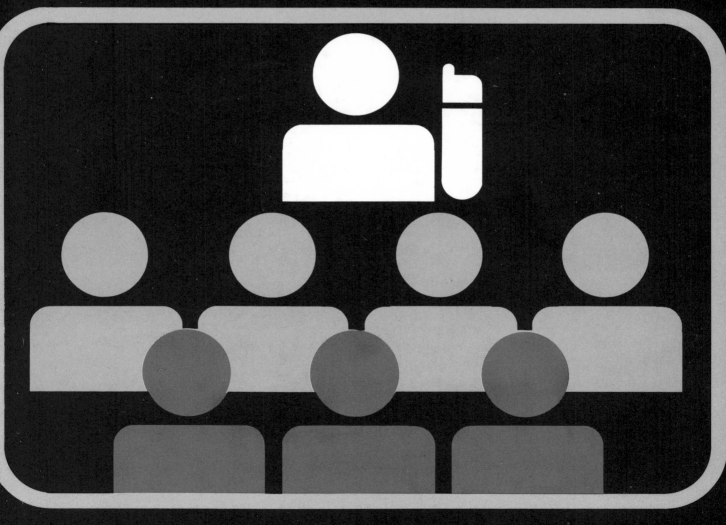

Thomas D. Morton and Ronald K. Green, Editors
Office of Continuing Social Work Education
School of Social Work
The University of Tennessee, Knoxville

Training in the Human Services

Papers presented at the
First National Conference on
TRAINING IN THE HUMAN SERVICES
The University of Tennessee School of Social Work
Gatlinburg, Tennessee – November 7-9, 1977

Training in the Human Services

Edited by
THOMAS D. MORTON
and
RONALD K. GREEN

The University of Tennessee
School of Social Work • Knoxville

ISBN 0-89695-002-6

Acknowledgements

The conference which spawned these papers and the actual preparation of this volume represent the dedicated efforts of many people. None of these efforts would have been possible without the support of Dean Ben Granger, who demonstrated his strong commitment to the development and exchange of new knowledge in this field by his willingness to back new ventures such as this one.

In the preparation and execution of the conference itself, thanks go to all OCSWE staff members who made themselves available whenever support was needed. Special acknowledgement should go to Mike Parker and Renee Gilbertson of the program staff who carried the responsibility for coordination and administration of the conference. The preparation of this volume was made possible by the willingness of the authors to commit their conference presentations to paper. As always, the extremely competent editorial staff at OCSWE, Mary Brashear, Mary Anne Blazek and Joyce Payne, was able to take manuscripts in various stages of completion and turn them into a publication accurately communicating the substance provided by the authors.

Contents

I. Introduction

In the introductory paper that follows, the editors of this volume discuss a series of issues and unanswered questions related to the current state of training in the human services. This is intended to provide a context for the remaining articles and to indicate the amount of effort needed to develop this field adequately.

The following problem issues and questions are discussed as to their impact on training efforts:

1. The unrealistic expectations often placed on trainers to solve organizational problems which may well be beyond the realistic scope of training.

2. The second class status often assigned to training efforts and staff, whether it be due to the failure to provide stable resources or failure to reward training efforts on the same basis as parallel organizational efforts.

3. The lack of well-developed mechanisms for human service training professionals to engage in exchanges of training practice.

4. The conflict between the expectations of organizational administrators and actual participants as to the objectives or goals of training.

5. The lack of well-developed evaluation technology.

6. The fact that the early developmental stages of human service practice poses problems to those responsible for development of training programs in this area.

In addition, the development of this volume and the rationale behind its organization and formating is discussed.

Training in the Human Services: Issues and Questions

by Thomas D. Morton and Ronald K. Green

Ronald K. Green, M.S., M.P.A., J.D., is Director of the Office of Continuing Social Work Education of the University of Tennessee School of Social Work. Thomas D. Morton, M.S.W., is Administrator of Continuing Social Work Education at the University of Georgia.

The training of human service practitioners represents a multimillion dollar annual operation. Employee participation in training programs adds to the total cost of public and private human service agencies in America. In addition to direct expenditures for programs in criminal justice, public social services under Title XX, mental health, vocational rehabilitation and other areas, agencies must absorb travel expenses, lost production time and the other indirect costs of training. Is the effort worthwhile? Aside from the issue of whether or not the money for training is well spent, there is little agreement on what the observable outcome of training should be.

Training has been said to be more an art than a science. Following this line of reasoning, one could also suggest that, like art, only time can judge the value of training. Yet, time may not display the same patience it has had with Piccaso or Van Gogh. There is little reason to believe that the trainer will be able to escape much longer the demands for evaluation and measures of effectiveness heard in other areas of the human services. Just as agencies and services are being forced to justify their continued existence by demonstrating their public impact, training programs may need to justify their continued existence by demonstrating their impact on the quality of an agency's service or on its effective utilization of resources.

Evaluation is just one of the many issues facing trainers in human services. This article raises a number of questions currently confronting trainers concerning training in the human services. While a few answers are given, the authors suggest that resolution of these questions is of immediate concern, both for trainers and for the agencies and programs which support them.

1. Training is subject to political and economic pressures which often result in unrealistically high expectations. Training is asked to solve a multitude of agency problems. In public welfare, recent federal audits in many states have revealed error rates resulting in the over expenditure of millions of dollars. One of the perceived causes of these errors was poorly trained staff, thereby justifying the large scale expansion of training activities designed to reduce error rates. While errors may be partially attributable to the lack of knowledge and skill of the person conducting an eligibility determination, other factors must also be considered. These include the morale and environment of the agencies, staff turnover, the validity of the information provided by the client, and the effectiveness of intrasystem linkages which support the entire service delivery system. Errors may be derived from misinterpretation of policy, erroneous mathematical computations, the use of erroneous or fraudulent data, or translation errors in communication from one component of the agency to another. Only one of these four sources of error can be corrected through intensified worker training in areas of policy.

Besides being two high, the expected outcomes of training are often ambiguous. A state correctional agency may undertake a broad scale training program in human relations. This training is somehow perceived as increasing or improving the quality of service delivered by correctional officers, probation staff and other professional care givers within the correctional system. Yet, what actually constitutes improvements in rates of performance or in the quality of care often escapes definition. One set of decision makers may expect human relations training to result in lower rates of recidivism or lower rates of client matriculation towards institutional settings. Whereas, another may perceive this training as affecting only the human quality of service, a value which may be distinctly separate from certain other productive outcomes. The real problem flows from the lack of clearly defined program objectives.

Finally, agency based training often suffers the same fate of ancillary services in public schools. While the budget is fat and funds are available, training programs flourish, but in times of economic severity, they are the first to be cut and the last to be renewed. The suggestion that training is considered a luxury rather than a necessity appears to be true.

2. <u>Trainers and training lack recognized legitimacy</u>. To a great extent, our lexicon relegates training to second class status, behind education. Consider these differences: we have college preparatory education and vocational training; we have formal education and in-service training. While it might be argued that these distinctions represent a differentiation in process between education and training, this argument breaks down. Persons who make the distinction between the processes of education and training perceive education as having a generalized focus with intended learning outcomes primarily at the level of chain learning

and concept formation. These same persons think that training is focused on the application of knowledge in specific situations and that the learning outcomes are at the level of transfer generalization and problem solving. In this frame of reference, one would receive training in accounting and be educated in mathematics, training in diagnostics and education in human behavior; training in law and education in political science.

In many instances, these distinctions are artificial. Many educational programs involve instructional components designed to teach application and problem solving and many training programs include instructional designs to teach concepts. Yet, in spite of the similarities in methodology, academic faculty often look askance at the trainers and training components of both human service agencies and their own university based programs. Academic, faculty are perceived to have acquired a state of competence through both experience and study, whereas trainers are often perceived to be technicians sliding by on minimal amounts of knowledge. Certain agency practices tend to support these stereotypes. The need to comply with civil service and other requirements often results in the overgeneralization of skills required to perform training and salaries at an artifically low level. Even when salaries are higher, training units must promote from within and face other constraints upon lateral entry. These factors make it difficult to hire trainers directly from the outside, thereby denying the training unit the flexibility to pursue higher levels of skill and experience.

Even agency-based trainers who have such skill and experience are often perceived by members of their own agency as imitation faculty. When discussing their training needs, many agency staff also request that the training be delivered by outside experts rather than their own training staff. These feelings are partially related to the colleague-turned-expert phenomenon in which a previous co-worker is now in the position of training others. Previous relationships with the trainer or knowledge of his/her background make it difficult for trainees to legitimize the new trainer's expertise.

Agency-based trainers may have further imperiled their legitimacy by trying to make themselves all things to all people and by attempting to deliver units of instruction in areas which are not part of their personal repertoire. Some trainers have been criticized for thinking that they can research any previously unknown topic and teach others all there is to know about it. While some trainers may be successful in these efforts, failure by others has served to damage the credibility of agency-based training staff.

Often, there is conflict between agency-based training efforts and university-based training efforts. For many years training funds at the federal level reflected legislative patterns which routed the money for training stage agency and local staff through universities. Agencies were at the mercy of the universities' inclination to respond to available federal funds or to allocate resources towards continuing education structures which would facilitate using available federal monies for training programs. There were often conflicts over the appropriateness of needs identification processes. Agencies argued that universities often wrote training grants to meet the needs and interests of their faculty, rather than the needs and realities of the state agency. Universities often countered that by virtue of their functions in the areas of research and the generation of new knowledge, they were in a better position to offer a future orientation regarding training. Universities further argued that it was not the role of the university to provide basic agency training, but rather to provide advanced level educational and training programs. The implication was that basic skill training should be provided by the agency or that persons should be recruited for agency positions, based on a prerequisite of these skills. From the agency perspective much university-based training is perceived as academic and not focused on practice.

These latter issues reflect a continuing conflict between agencies and universities regarding the role of one versus that of the other in in-service training. Under Title XX, many universities, schools of social work and related programs are now finding themselves offering in noncredit forms of instruction many of the basic components of their BSW and MSW curriculums. Some faculty are concerned that they may be undermining their commitment to professional social work education. Certainly Title XX funding patterns, along with the trend toward greater state agency control over mental health training funds, will result in university-delivered training which more accurately reflects the perceived needs of the agency.

Human service trainers in all settings, academic and agency, are generally isolated from each other. In many agencies, trainers are few in number; in some agencies there may be only one. This limits the possibility for collegial interaction and exchange of practice. Further, since trainers are invariably tied to a specific type of service delivery agency, they are often limited in their affiliations. There is little cross pollination between trainers in corrections, mental health, public social services, aging, health or other areas of human service practice. In part this reflects the primary allegiance of trainers to the field of practice in which they work. It also shows that trainers as a constituency are linked by similar function. While they represent a natural constituency, the constituency is very fragmented. National conferences in the field of corrections, public welfare, child welfare, aging and other areas, often devote only minimal portions of the programs to activities which would be of interest to trainers. When such content is included on the program, it is often directed towards exchanging descriptive information about the content of training programs, rather than on methodological content which might facilitate the advancement of the trainer's instructional skills. Further solidifying their isolation is the reality that many agencies do not provide funds for trainers to attend conferences. The economy of scale is often such that there is no perceived cost benefit in providing extensive training to agency-based trainers when the entire training unit consists of two or three trainers.

Human service trainers lack adequate mediums for exchanging practice information. Most training programs are never published or reproduced for distribution. In many cases the format is designed for one particular group. It may be delivered by a trainer on only two or three occasions. Since the trainer is often in the position of preparing instructional materials only for his own use there is often little descriptive material available which would help another trainer replicate the the program. Available materials are generally in the form of handouts, agendas or course outlines and, in some cases, reproduced journal articles. More sophisticated packages of materials are often produced in limited quantities and are intended for the trainee population only. This limits the access of other potential users and makes it difficult to gain from the work of others.

Training efforts do not lend themselves to journal articles and it is often difficult to select an appropriate journal for those that do. Although

the Journal of the American Society for Training and Development is devoted
to training, its focus and constituency in many ways does not reflect the
resource realities and constraints of human service agencies and related
training programs. Other journals are more interested in training-affiliated
research than in specific descriptive information on instructional design
or detailed description of methods of instruction and curriculum. National
conferences seldom provide an adequate format for the exchange of practice
on training, since few trainers attend. The major focus of the conference
program is on substantive issues (e.g., mental illness, child welfare,
aging, social work education, behavior therapy, etc.), and the concerns of
training practitioners and professionals become a peripheral consideration
in this arena.

Trainers are caught in the ideological conflict between process and
goal orientation. In the 1960's, approaches to training were significantly
influenced by the increasing popularity of behavioral theory. Stretching
into the early 1970's, the writings of Skinner, Gagne, Piaget and others
caused both trainers and educators to turn their attention to the technology
of instruction. However, during the early seventies, the increasing popularity
of androgogy or adult learning theory resulted in a process orientation
towards instructional design. The earlier writers emphasized concerns
related to the sequencing of instruction, factors associated with the
presentation of stimulus, reinforcement, and dimensions of cognitive association. Writers in the later period emphasized process considerations, such
as the involvement of the learner in assessing his own needs and the significant attention paid to the comfort and perceived emotional security of the
learning environment. Zealots on both sides have served to produce an
artificial dichotomy between the two approaches. Ultimately learning is

both a product of the technology of instruction and the processes surrounding its operation.

One of the principal tenets of androgogy is that the learner should assess his own needs rather than having needs assigned to him. Certainly, sociological research on innovations indicates that the rate of adoption is enhanced by goal identification and acceptance. Goal identification and acceptance is enhanced if the target population participates in the determination of the goal. Yet, for the agency, this presents its own brand of conflict. Since administration and management are largely responsible for the delineation of roles and the assignment of tasks, one might argue that the agency should also be responsible for the determination of requisite skills for accomplishing these tasks. It would follow then, that the agency has a legitimate right to determine the substance, nature and scope of training endeavors. Countering this is the argument that persons in any agency role are closest to the demands of their unique set of functions and, therefore, are best able to describe their needs in relation to performing the task assigned them. In the continual battle between perceived and attributed needs, who is in the best position to determine the "real" need?

Evaluation of training efforts is both costly and difficult. In many instances funders expect sophisticated training evaluation programs without structurally allowing for this in both the design and funding of the project. This phenomenon is even experienced in the research and evaluation oriented organization such as NIMH. While some components of skill and knowledge acquisition can be measured immediately following a learning experience, it is also true that learning can confront a set of circumstances for several weeks which cause him to make the proper set of associations required for understanding a concept or for putting it into practice. Further, it is impossible to measure the degree or extent to which the trainee utilizes knolwedge and skill acquired in training sessions until a reasonable period has passed and the trainee has had an opportunity to confront a situation requiring the use of these items. Many training programs and projects are designed so that the funding stops immediately upon the completion of the training and without any provision for longitudinal follow-up. In an attempt to maximize the delivery of instruction to the highest number of trainees and to minimize the per-unit cost of instruction, resources available for evaluation often preclude the possibility of sound evaluation design.

Circumstance which make the evaluation of human service programs difficult also make the evaluation of human service training programs difficult. It is impossible to construct training designs that allow for random selection of trainees, control groups or other features that are desirale from the perspective of sound research.

Finally, evaluation of training programs is hampered by the inability of relevant parties to agree upon and designate training outcomes in observable performance tests. Even when we are able to specify the expected competencies, the technology for measuring these competencies is insufficient or the cost of using such procedures is prohibitive. While the quality of instructional objectives for training programs has improved in recent years, there has not been a corresponding increase in the rate of evaluation of these instructional objectives.

Human service trainers are limited by the nature of the technology in the fields in which they work. One of the realities of human service organizations is that their technology is generally indeterminate. Technology is based on a body of knowledge that insures, within certain limits, the success of the transformation process enabling the training of personnel to perform the necessary tasks. The level of determinancy of the technology is a function of three major variables: (1) the extent to which the desired outcomes are tangible and well defined; (2) the degree of stability of the raw material; and (3) the depth of knowledge available about cause and effect relationships and the raw material. For the most part, human service organizations operate under theories or service ideologies which constitute proposed, but not validated, explanations of client problems. Our lack of knowledge in many areas of human service delivery and managment of human service organizations leaves the trainer with precise but limited techniques which he/she can convey to the trainee population. Trainees often demand training content which is immediately relevant with a high degree of procedural specificity. When trainers succumb to these demands, they inevitably provide trainees with oversimplifications or overgeneralizations. Yet, to resist these demands is to be accused of providing information which is too theoretical and impractical.

In part, this problem reflects the old conflict between concepts and skills. Discussion of these two items as separate entities connotes some level of disimilarity. Yet, practicality suggests that problem solving is the application of previously learned principles to novel situations. Concepts are discreet items and principles, on the other hand, are a chaining of concepts. From a learning perspective, skills and concepts are closely intertwined, just as theory is built from practice and practice is based upon the application of theory.

These and similar issues generated the First Fall Conference on Training in the Human Services. The conference was perceived as a medium through which both agency and university based trainers in human service arenas might exchange practice and, in so doing, learn from each other; mutually address and identify issues and barriers to their practice; and take steps to enhance the quality of training activities in the human services. Participation was invited on a national basis. On November 1977, trainers from 27 states, the District of Columbia, and Canada convened in Gatlinburg, Tennessee to accomplish these ends. The list of attendees reflected a 50-50 mix of university and agency-based trainers. Ninety percent of the focus was on the training of human service practitioners in an on-the-job setting as opposed to generalized long-term professional education efforts in educational institutions.

Following the conference, presenters were asked to submit papers based on their presentations. The papers in this volume represent the practice ideas which were shared at the First Fall Conference on Training in Human Services.

As the presentations and papers were reviewed, they seemed to fall into four categories. These are reflected in the two-dimensional matrix, illustrated in figure one.

FIGURE 1

	Design	Implementation
Training Technique		
Process		

The papers in this volume are organized accordingly. The matrix is not offered as a theoretical model, but rather as an emergence model based on material presented at the conference. Some papers focused on techniques of needs assessment, curriculum design, delivery of instruction or evaluation.

Others focused on the process through which certain activities were carried out. Both the technique and process orientations seem to distinguish themselves by different phases of the training effort. The phases were separated into two categories, design and implementation. It is recognized that no categorization exactly mirrors reality and that not all the papers fit neatly into this matrix, but it is offered as an aide in approaching the broad range of material provided in this volume.

The papers present the work of the authors themselves and their compilation of the words and thoughts of others. They represent an open communication of thoughts among colleagues. They are offered as a further advancement of the major goal for the First Fall Conference on Training and the Human Services, an exchange of practice.

II. The Design of Training Processes

The papers in this section focus on the design of training processes. Paul Abels suggests a basic philosophy which should underlie training in human services in his discussion of a value-based synergistic approach to training. Thomas Cruthirds deals with how agencies can greatly multiply their staff training efforts by teaching their existing first and second line supervisors to establish continuing staff development programs. Finally, Pat Dunn and Ernest Kahn describe the process of developing a program evaluation training curriculum for a state public social service system.

Abels proposes a philosophical base for training which considers the basic values of the professional promotion of justice, dignity and freedom. He calls for development of a synergistic approach to training; one in which trainer and worker engage in a process of communication to seek a radical effective solution to problems even though they may start with differing views about what is the best solution. The goal is to find a mutually satisfying solution—a win/win solution rather than one that completely satsifies only one participant or neither (such as in the case of a compromise). Abels also discusses how difficult this is, since our culture tends to promote an I win/you lose approach. He suggests ways in which an agency might adopt the synergistic model.

Based on the observation that agency supervisory staff members are greatly underutilized as teachers of new staff, Cruthirds discusses how supervisors can be educated to assume much greater teaching roles. He discusses the prevailing bias against heavy use of supervisory staff as teachers, for such reasons as lack of time, lack of formal substantive knowledge, and lack of knowledge and skill in training.

Cruthirds then discusses the efficiency that potentially could be gained if agencies adopted a formal program for giving supervisors the necessary substantive knowledge and educational theory to carry out the educational role.

Cruthirds discusses the Vantage Point project, in which supervisors in the Tennessee Department of Human Services received training with first-line staff. The specific methodology used for training supervisors to teach is reviewed and the need for administrative support is discussed.

Drew and Kahn describe the process of developing a training program on program evaluation for public social service staff in New Jersey. The authors discuss in some detail the basic principles on which the training curriculum was developed.

1. All levels of staff need to be involved.

2. Different levels need to have different information.

3. Rules and functions of different staff need to be clarified.

4. Lack of a single model of evaluation obviates against a single training model.

5. Diversity of models requires adaptation of any one system of materials.

They then discuss the actual curriculum developed which included three courses, one on evaluation research for program and evaluation staff, one on the administrative model of program evaluation for administrative staff, and one on staff development for evaluation for staff development staff. They conclude with a discussion of the realities of implementing this type of evaluation training model.

Synergistic Training

by Paul Abels

Paul Abels, Ph.D., is Associate Dean and Professor of Social Work at Case Western Reserve University in Cleveland, Ohio.

INTRODUCTION

If I were to look at the major purposes which underlie the existence of a group of people who call themselves human service workers, it would be to help build a just society in which people could live in freedom and dignity. By dignity, I would mean that all people are equally worthy and should be treated with respect. No one is more worthy--worker, client, professor, student, president, etc. All people are equally worthy of respect. By freedom I mean: (1) the enhancement of human development to its fullest; (2) the right to privacy; and (3) autonomy, the ability to have a range of alternatives from which to choose and to know that there is some possibility that these choices can be achieved.[1]

In looking at the training decisions I make or that we might make together as a learning group, it would be vital to assess whether the consequences of our actions lead to a just society, to social justice. Not only is this the vision I believe people seek in our profession but it relates in a broad way to our profession's mission.

Normative Training

Since I am suggesting that these consequences "ought" to be the basis of our actions, I am proposing a normative approach to training.

1. The major question is always what ought to be, if the consequences are to be what is good or right. What actions are most likely to lead to the goals of a just society. What action "A" under what conditions "C" leads to desired results "R." These are our goals--or contract if you will--which form the basis for a normative approach.

2. The structure of our practice environment, whether it be classroom, agency or business, needs to minimize the nature of the alienating forces which categorizes most of our institutions. Not only do decisions have to be made openly, democratically, knowledgably and reflectively, but they have to have the commitment, engagement and action of those who are involved with the consequences. What structure leads to the best consequences for people? Can an agency or a school of social work become a just community?

3. The base of knowledge with which we operate has been borrowed from other groups. Although this has provided important flexibility, all the consequences have not been positive.

   a. We have minimized our own research.

   b. Much of the social science we use is worthless because it lacks practicality, middle class or student sample pool, and because it is not comparative or grounded.

   c. As the fields from which we borrowed discard their own early approaches, we find ourselves without a foundation to call our own. We must, therefore, find our own knowledge and have it grounded in our own practice. Training, supervision and practice must all reflect our own unique contributions and value system.

   d. In a world of what ought to be, decisions should be made in ways which do not put down people--a "win/win" situation rather than "I win/you lose"--or "I have the power, therefore, do as I say."

   e. Finally, an outgrowth of a normative approach needs to be an emphasis on the self help view--whether with clients, community or the university--we need to use leaders and professionals, but we should not come to depend on them. We need to help people find the resources within themselves wherever possible.

Synergistic Processes

The very best in agency practice requires that trainers bring out the very best in the staff. Crucial to this process is the humanistic connection integrating the client, worker and supervisor with the administrator and trainer. The nature of the connections between the trainer and the learner is a crucial factor in determining the amount of growth that can occur in the field. If there is mutual trust, respect and acceptance of each other's dignity, it matters not whether the instructor is always knowledgable of alternative solutions, or whether the learner's actions are always correct. The term "synteraction" will suggest the process of communication which permits this advanced variation to take place. It provides a receptive medium or culture in which growth can take place and in which the individual feels a response from other parts of the system which are "sympatico."

We will define synergy as the melding of two or more conflicting points of view into one which is more creative or better than any single suggestion would have been. Synergy is the joint search for truth, an inquiry into how two or more people, often with differing views of what the answer might be, can find a radical-effective solution to a problem. The need for this synergising environment is particularly vital in situations where the nature of the worker-client interaction exacerbates the environmental press on the worker and/or the client.

Synergy suggests that when each party in the transaction maintains somewhat selfish thinking (what's best for me and the agency), the result will be of a higher order than if each looks at what is only best for himself. The task becomes one of finding a mutually satisfying solution. Maslow suggests that "self-actualizing people rise above the dichotomy between selfishness and unselfishness."[2]

In essence we are not considering what is best for any one segment of the subsystem, but what is best for all involved. As a supervisor, for example, my extrapersonal communication might be, "If by attempting to modify the system I can help the worker and agency (worker and myself), then I have come up with a result which rewards everyone." Admittedly these solutions are difficult in a complex society or system, but, in part, they are so difficult for us because: (1) the nature of our culture implies an "I win/you lose" approach; and (2) we have not learned to take synergistic approaches.

Changes in culture, however, are taking place and the concept of synergy has grown in importance in the work of psychologists such as Abraham Maslow and "world viewers" such as Buckminster Fuller.[2]

Synergy As A Tool For Growth--Survival

If one were to take innovation as a metaphor for growth and survival the coupling bond (or the marriage bond), one would have in the nature of the reproductive process a model for synergy. Without the linkage of new genetic materials the possibilities for innovation are lost. The group becomes whole through growth and in fact enhances its own extinction by not accepting the new.

It is the synergistic approach, whether in the learner teacher relationship, staff meetings, or committee work that permits innovations in the agency. It is the ability to take in new ideas and build on them which provides variation in approach and eventually in the nature of the staff.

If all workers were to remain fixed in their ideas or were required to adopt the ideas of the supervisor or the agency director, not only would there be a lack of growth in their ability to function as autonomous workers, but the level of growth of the agency would likewise suffer. Clearly, setting the culture of the agency on a high synergy level not only benefits staff growth but also serves agency survival. In the long run--in competition with agencies that are more flexible, creative, and able to use innovative, high synergy approaches--agency survival may require, in fact demand, a synergistic approach to administration.

I am suggesting, therefore, that the adoption on an agency-wide basis of a commitment to a synergistic growth environment would provide the following.

1. Benefit the learner, by permitting and structuring autonomous, creative growth.

2. Minimize the bosslike qualities of supervision and training, which often force good social workers to become bad teachers and permit the trainer to grow as a human being.

3. Mobilize a force of workers for the agency who are creative, excited and constantly moving to higher levels of performance.

4. Benefit the clients by providing innovative attempts to help and giving them a sense of being worked with in a synergistic manner.

<u>The consequences would be a highly creative and effective agency in which all people would be treated with respect and dignity and would be free to develop.</u>

What might the steps be for setting the proper agency culture for a synergy model? Let's explore some possibilities. The first step might be to specify the goals that a model might offer and to contract with the trainers to use the approach, whether agency-wide or as a trial, limited to a set of workers who fell akin to its ideas.

The second step would be to acknowledge that the actions of any party in interaction are reinforcing and that the thrust of these actions is in the best interest of the client, the improved practice of the worker, or the best administrative action. In fact, they are partners in the quest for a synergistic solution.

The third agreement is that compromise is unacceptable. When differences arise concerning approach, both parties must try to overcome the dichotomy and not to profit from the conflict.

Deadlock is most likely to occur in those areas in which your opinion seems as good as mine but I think my way is better; or areas in which I feel I have been threatened and must cope by defending myself. At those points I may resort to emotion and avoid working toward a solution. A committment to synergistic approaches brings me back to the cause of mutuality, a more efficient and fulfilling method of problem solving. In this respect, it is hooked into the normative approach, a quest for the true solution based on the quest for additional evidence.

As a process, synteraction reflects the changes taking place in people's perceptions of what the nature of the working relationship should be. As Carl Rogers, among others, has pointed out, we are entering into the era of the "new man (woman too)."[3] This person deplores sham, rejects tradition, does not fit the "traditional industrial and organizational model," doesn't fit into the military, will not put up with double-talk, and reacts negatively to controls and authoritarianism. Others have suggested that there is a push toward self-management; experiments with various work models in England and on the kibbutzim seem to bear out the success of the new person and the new models.

These new models will be evident in the social work profession as they are already in the life-styles of the people that social workers deal with. There is a new person in the nature of the client, in the nature of the problems which he presents and in the nature of the contract that he is willing to make in order to obtain help. He wants in on the contract, whether it is the mechanism of "maximum feasible participation" or the demand for a nonsexist therapist. There is growing recognition that traditional institutions not only are in need of change but are indeed changing.

A Synergistic Polarity

Our western way of thinking tends to see things in absolutes. Our positions are usually right, our opponents are wrong; our ideas are good, the others are bad. Naturally, if we all operate from that point of view at staff meetings, it would be beneficial for me to negate your ideas in order to minimize the apparent importance of opposing suggestions.

There are certain approaches that the supervisor and the group can experiment with which may help them restructure their patterns of thinking and doing. Efforts to promote openness to ideas led to the development of brain storming techniques and the Spectrum Approach, developed by G. M. Prince.[4] Prince felt that generally people attack new ideas based on traditional fight/flight patterns. They do this by searching out the bad part of an idea and then attempt to destroy the total idea. He has evolved a process in which the members must deal with the good part of the idea and build from there.

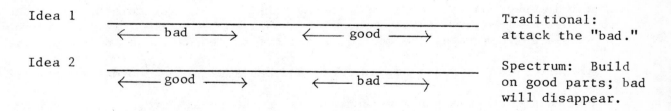

This is similar to the Taoist philosophy of becoming one with the thrust of the other, rather than opposing it. What is the person attempting to achieve? How can I as supervisor help rather than oppose? This can lead to a synergistic solution; the ideas are now group worked ideas and their potential value is clear when the specific idea choice needs to be made. The procedure restructures the thinking processes in ways which alter traditional patterns. The use of analogy, metaphor and teaching stories also permit this kind of restructuring. Our introductory cat story represents a traditional teaching method used by the Sufis. The story has meaning on various levels and permits the learner to tune into what he is ready for. Idries Shah, discussing such Sufi tales, suggests the story "may be understood at any one of many depths. There is the joke, the moral, and the little extra which brings the consciousness...a little further on the way to realization."[5]

The use of analogies, comparisons with nature or mechanical objects is part of a creative problem solving process, "synectics," by which traditional thinking patterns might be modified. The question "what is the similarity between the concept of acceptance and an electric toaster?" opens new ways of thinking which don't require expertise in "acceptance."

A Paradigm For Our Time

Staff who are attempting to develop their capacities for helping are part of a vast network of interrelated acts, past, present and future, which impact on both their clients and themselves. The more holistic the view staff can take, the more relevant the action can be on behalf of the client. That is, the more one sees and deals with the context, the more one relates to the total person. This is the model for our time--a normative-ecological approach which deals with the person as part of a system. In our times, practice which recognizes the power of this approach can lend hope to the people, providing the trainer can compose the structural complex in a way that permits staff to find a small enough piece of the pattern to deal with.

Kurt Lewin's force field analysis offers such a perspective.[7] On a linear plain, it permits one to view all the parts of the system, including external forces. Lewin proposed the following. (1) Any social situation can be perceived as being in a state of equilibrium, or balance, at any point in time, and the nature of that equilibrium can be assessed. Current staff functioning for example is held in equilibrium by a number of opposing forces which are equal in total strength. (2) Certain forces are at work which promote learning and doing in a new way (change). These are the driving forces: a desire to do a good job, recognition, potential for growth, supervision, attending classes, an open mind. (3) Certain forces are at work which retard change. These are the restrining forces: heavy job load, busy supervisor, fear of the new, stereotyping, or traditional patterns of behavior. For example, Hare points out that "Some supervisors saw peer group supervision as an attack on their worth."[8] This is a restraining force that would need to be worked out. (4) In addition, there are certain blocks which are neutral but still influence the worker: building size, budget, laws.

Theoretically, if the current level of functioning is in balance, an alteration in either of the driving or restraining forces should alter that balance. The addition of another driving force, or the elimination of a restraining force should help the supervisory group move closer to the goals of improved practice.

Force field analysis can be done over a period of months in an agency analysis or it can be done in five minutes prior to meeting with a supervisee.

It helps maintain a focus on the tasks to be performed. By maintaining a "point of concentration" on the specific piece of the problem to be solved, even large problems can be partialized and dealt with. This point of concentration must be maintained by all the group members when problem solving.[9] The group itself can explore the forces for and against change and decide which factor can provide leverage for change.

CONCLUSION

Any process which permits a holistic view in a sense comes close to the synergistic mode. That is why an ecological or a systems view permits us to grasp the implications of our actions. In a brilliant metaphoric novel "Mount Analog" we are told how our hero, while mountain climbing one day, kills a mouse, this upsets the ecological balance which erodes the soil and in turn causes an avalanche which kills some other mountain climbers. He is banished from ever climbing again.[10] In the same novel the author states:

> "When you strike off on your own, leave some trace of your passage which will guide you coming back: one stone set on another, some grass weighted by a stick. But if you come to an impasse or a dangerous spot, remember that the trail you have left could lead people coming after you into trouble. So go back along your trail and obliterate any traces you have left. This applies to anyone who wishes to leave some mark of his passage in the world. Even without wanting to, you always leave a few traces. Be ready to answer to your fellow men for the trail you leave behind you."

> And You, What Do You Seek?

FOOTNOTES

1. For a more comprehensive view of these concepts, see Steven Lukes, Individualism (New York: Harper Torchbooks, 1973); and Paul Abels, The New Supervision and Staff Development (New York: Association Press, 1977).

2. Abraham Maslow, Eupsychian Management (Homewood, Illinois: Dorsey Press, 1965); R. Buckminster Fuller, Synergistics (New York: MacMillan, 1975).

3. Carl R. Rogers, "The Person of Tomorrow," Sonoma State College Commencement Address, June 7, 1969.

4. G. M. Prince, The Practice of Creativity (New York: Collier Books, 1968).

5. Indries Shah, The Sufis (New York: Anchor Books, 1964), p. 63.

6. D. Koberg and J. Bagnell, The Universal Traveler (Los Altos: Kaufman, 1972); and William J. Gordon, Synectics (New York: Collier Books, 1961).

7. Kurt Lewin, "Group Decision and Social Change," in Readings in Social Psychology, O. Swanson, M. Newcomb and E. Hartley, editors (New York: Host, 1952).

8. R. T. Hare and S. Franklin, "Peer Group Supervision," American Journal of Orthopsychiatry, Vol. 42, No. 3, 1972, pp. 527-529.

9. Viola Spolin, Improvisation for the Theatre (Chicago: Northwestern University Press, 1963).

10. Rene Daumal, Mount Analogue (San Francisco: City Lights Books, 1959).

Educating Supervisors
To Assume Their Teaching Role

by Thomas Cruthirds

Thomas Cruthirds, D.S.W., is Associate Professor at the University of Tennessee School of Social Work, Knoxville Branch.

The Irony of Supervision

In the field of social welfare, and particularly within the social services, perhaps the most impressive reservoir of professional talent can be found in the first and second line supervisory cadre. This "talent lode" resides, by and large, among career specialists in child welfare, rehabilitation, family service, medical social work, school social work, mental health, aging, corrections, and other rather sharply defined fields of practice. Usually, these professionals have advanced through the caseworker or counseling ranks, are committed through strong ties to their particular field, and aspire to lengthy supervisory careers. In short, this group of professionals provides a valuable degree of stability and continuity within the social services. They are a group to be reckoned with.

Most of these supervisors preserve their equanimity in the face of often devastating pressures. New staff may inadequately prepared for their direct service responibilities and may be placed at once under conditions of severe professional overload. A common consequence of this situation is "worker burn-out"[1] with ensuing high rates of staff turnover, particularly in large metropolitan areas. The supervisor, of course, may again be faced with the task of orienting new personnel to fuel the engine of service. Or, if replacements are not readily available, the supervisor herself may be required to step in and maintain caseload contact.

The tenure and stability of the supervisory cadre is often in striking contrast to the sometimes temporary and even transient direct service population. The supervisor may be the only guarantee of ongoing knowledge about the agency and its mission, the community and its needs, the unique imperatives of the field of practice, the diverse caseload, and the precise needs and abilities of staff. This group of career supervisors plays a pivotal role in most fields of practice in the social services.

It is ironic that supervisors, often so well prepared by virtue of their experience, are so underutilized as teachers within their own fields of practice. The main theme developed here is that the supervisor in the social services may well have some of the best potential for teaching casework skill, technique, values, and attitudes in direct case practice. An attempt to educate supervisors to assume their teaching role will be described and discussed. Thoughts about the efficacy of such a strategy of staff development will be examined.

Staff Development—The Usual Way

It has long been recognized that a certain limited training role is inherent in social services supervision.[2] However, the responsibility for providing the bulk of formal in-service training in direct case practice is usually carried by persons other than the agency's first or second line supervisors. Such training may be organized and delivered in a variety of

ways--by staff from the agency's training division; by program specialist
staff having policy responsibility for certain services; by directors of
professional services within large agencies; by university faculty and/or
continuing education personnel; by staff of specialized private research,
development, and training institutes; and by individual private consultants.[3]
Especially in the public social services, much of the recent training has
been organized through contracts with outside groups, often through provisions
of Titles IV and XX of the Social Security Act, as amended. These nonsuper-
visory, nonagency personnel are largely responsible for teaching casework
to caseworkers and supervision to supervisors.

The reasons for this state of affairs are, of course, complex and
difficult to specify. They are, however, related to what seem to be certain
prevailing assumptions about the inadvisability of depending too heavily
upon first and second line supervisors to carry the central training responsibility within social organizations. The "prevailing wisdom" (often even
articulated by supervisors themselves) can be summarized.

1.   Too heavy an involvement in training will result in the
      supervisor having insufficient time to devote to other
      important aspects of the job, especially managerial
      case quality control.

2.   The supervisor is unlikely, in many cases, to possess
      sufficient formal knowledge about direct practice, required
      of those who would be qualified to teach such content and
      skills.

3.   The supervisor is unlikely to have appropriate education
      or experience in the methodology of teaching, it could not
      be offered in a systematic and effective manner.

4.   The blend of requisite knowledge and teaching ability is
      most likely to be found in those already carrying teaching
      responsibilities (trainers, faculty, consultants, etc.), so
      that teaching specialists provide the greatest cost effectiveness.

As one might expect, agency management often espouses this first
consideration, agency training and staff development personnel seem to

stress assumptions two and three, while contract trainers and faculty would find favor with the final point. At any rate, the weight of this thinking, along with the reluctance of many first and second line supervisors to contradict openly the established scheme of things, serves to reinforce the usual pattern of training in the social services.

Some Misgivings about the Prevailing Logic

Although it is uncommon to rely on service supervisors as primary teachers of direct case service practitioners, some tantalyzing questions continue to surface. Is it necessarily the case that heavy teaching responsibility would detract from the case quality control management aspect of supervision? Is it not possible that supervisor-led training could provide a regular vehicle for in-depth group discussion of particular cases, thereby leading to an increase in case quality in the workers? Couldn't it be possible that supervisory time spent in training could be ordered so as to serve directly, in a planned way, the quality control imperative?

And if the agency is concerned that its supervisors are not technically qualified to teach direct case practice, would there be a way to remedy this condition? What if placing formal training responsibility on the services supervisor resulted in a pattern of personal study and preparation in contemporary theory of direct practice? Couldn't the agency reinforce this supervisory readiness to learn by providing educational leave opportunities and contract training in direct case management specifically designed for supervisory audiences? Wouldn't the agency's supervisors be able to relate this knowledge directly to the caseloads for which they are responsible?

If it is believed that supervisors have insufficient education or experience in the methodology of teaching, why couldn't this learning deficit be directly addressed? Why couldn't contract training resources be used for ongoing opportunities in which supervisors would be taught to teach? Learning theory, teaching methodology, techniques of guided group discussion, and many other methods could be profitably offered. This would be taught in the context of the supervisor's understanding of the mission of the agency.

Are we so certain that relevant knowledge about the specific field of practice, and appropriate teaching ability, can be systematically delivered for agency staff training through contract arrangements with universities, institutes and individual consultants? Is it not widely known that university faculty often are not educated in the basics of teaching methodology and technique? Is it not possible that faculty (and institute staff and consultants) might gradually divorce themselves from direct association with practice and thus diminish their effectiveness as teachers in particular areas? Is there not increasing concern that university faculty in professional fields may never have experienced direct case practice responsibilities?

If university faculty and consultants can become divorced from practice, couldn't the same phenomenon occur with agency training staff or substantive program specialist staff? Of course, the age-old question must be raised as to the ability of persons without experience in discrete fields (such as child protective services or probation and parole) to deliver valid training in such specializations. If the agency trainer is so extended in responsibility, is it not possible that the training rendered would run the risk of being peripheral to the central needs of direct service staff?

When these questions are considered, there are sufficient grounds to question the prevailing logic against using the supervisory cadre to mount and deliver primary, ongoing training within human service organizations. Indeed, one might present the contrary view--that given sufficient support, encouragement, and opportunity, the supervisor in the social services setting may prove to be the most able to take on the direct case service teaching role. The supervisor is potentially capable of providing exemplary training that "makes sense" in terms of the imperatives of the field,[4] because of continuing proximity to the unfolding pattern of case episodes, an intimate knowledge of the unit of caseworkers or counselors and their unique pressures and opportunities, and a strong identification with and commitment to the service philosphy of her particular agency. Further, it is possible that the key position occupied by the supervisor would encourage an interest in training to parallel interests in research in new service strategies and the development of more precise intervention techniques in specific fields. In this manner, research, development and training might well become linked and permanently imbedded within the core of the service agency.

Vantage Point--Teaching Materials for Supervisors

While the preceding notions about the training role of the supervisor are merely speculative at this point, there is basis for cautious optimism because of recent experience along such lines. In 1975 the author directed a statewide child welfare staff training project in direct case service management, on a contract basis, for the Tennessee Department of Human Services. Approximately 800 caseworkers and supervisors received consultant-led workshop training. Among the results of this training endeavor was a recommendation to

> "Develop video tape materials depicting actual
> client-worker and worker-supervisor interviews.
> Convert these materials into a format that can
> be used in preservice and in-service training
> and staff development, utilizing supervisory
> staff as the training cadre."[5]

This recommendation was the result of two prime considerations. First, retrenchment within the Department's Training Division had led to an organization-wide strategy of reliance on supervisory personnel to carry increasing training responsibilities at the local level. Second, experience in the TCPT training project had pointed to the often transitory quality of contract training, where high rates of staff turnover may tend to nullify much of the positive effects of training. What was needed was a project in which valid educational materials could be developed for the ongoing use of service supervisors—materials to be left within the agency at the conclusion of the project, along with a methodology for their use, so that training could be replicated as needed by the agency's own staff. What was wanted was a legacy of training material and methodology that would exist beyond the life of a given project, and that would contribute to the capacity of the organization to provide consistent training for its own personnel.

Out of these considerations was born the Vantage Point Series.[6] Vantage Point consists of two consecutive materials development and staff training projects which have produced "original scene"[7] color video tape training modules, along with referenced training guides, expressly for the use of supervisors in training staff for direct service work in child protective services,[8] and day care.[9] The child protective services training tapes consist of seven complete casework interviews, the corresponding supervisory conferences in six of these cases, along with video taped commentary of differential use of both casework and supervisory technique, skill, and process by several nationally-recognized consultants (including Harry Aponte, Alfred Kadushin, Leontine Young, and Alexander Zaphiris). The day care training tapes consist of original scene interactions in infant day care, preschool day care, school-age day care, and in-home day care; these, too, include video taped consultant commentary on technique and skill development.[10]

The production and refinement of these materials during 1976-77 is an exciting story in itself, having taken place in urban and rural areas in all parts of Tennessee. However, the more important aspect of the Vantage Point Series is the resulting development of a methodology through which the materials are used in teaching social services supervisors to teach direct case service skill and technique.

A Methodology for Teaching Supervisors To Teach

After the Vantage Point video tapes and training guides were developed in rough form, the materials were field tested by supervisors in various Tennessee locations. During these field tests the supervisors carried sole responsibility for providing training for their service units. Knowledge gained through observation of these early training attempts was used to revise and refine the recommended Vantage Point training methodology. Subsequently, eight regional workshops were held (each two to three days in length) in which eight to 40 supervisors simultaneously received training from our staff in the use of these materials. A total of 200 service supervisors were prepared through these workshops during the spring of 1977.

A major goal of the workshops was to see how quickly the participants would be able to supplant the Vantage Point staff from responsibility for the training role, and from responsibility for evaluating training strategy and efficacy. A key feature of the design was the cultivation of an open, direct pattern of criticism of the participants' training style (including that of the Vantage Point staff). Several assumptions gave direction to this training effort.

1. Service supervisors, by virtue of their position, education and experience, would have already had some experience in the teaching role.

2. By virtue of their substantive knowledge (in this case child protective services), familiarity with supervising direct service staff and knowledge of specific case examples, the supervisors would likely qualify as "experts" in their field.

3. To recognize, in a positive manner, their substantive expertise and previous teaching experience would enhance the possibility that the Vantage Point training would be viewed as additive (rather than repetitive) and thus both reinforce supervisors' belief in their own ability to teach and encourage a readiness to learn a new approach.

4. Each teacher or trainer would likely develop and employ a unique personal training style, as a natural consequence of creative thought.

5. There would be no prescribed way to conduct training, as variations and innovations in methodology, technique and strategy would possibly flourish because of the latitude inherent in our use of "original scenes" from direct case practice.

6. As various approaches to training were demonstrated before the group, valuable peer learning would occur, and as training progressed, peer influence would become accelerated and cumulative.

7. Successful attempts to teach within the relatively controlled workshop setting would reinforce the supervisors' desire to employ the Vantage Point materials and methodology in subsequent "real" staff development episodes.

The workshop training trajectory moved gradually from vicarious to actual experience in the development of teaching skill and technique. The progression followed this order: (1) Reading and Thinking. The preassigned training guide included material on training technology, as well as on various aspects of child protective services intervention. (2) Listening and Discussing. Vantage Point trainers explained certain concepts and utilized guided discussion, particularly in relation to training guide content. (3) Observing and Commenting. Trainees were placed temporarily in the role of direct service workers, as Vantage Point staff demonstrated methodology in the use of one of the video tapes in a mock training exercise. (4) Planning and Practicing. Trainees worked in small groups for lengthy periods to screen assigned videotapes and develop their own training formats. (5) Delivering a Training Episode. Trainees assumed the role of trainer, presenting time-limited training vignettes to the entire assemblage. (6) Evaluating and Critiquing. Trainees regularly critiqued both their own and others' training efforts, searching for group solutions to particular problems in training. (7) Engaging in Forward Planning. Trainees discussed in detail opportunities and problems associated with imbedding the Vantage Point training technology within the constraints of the agency.

Direct observation and written participant evaluation have led to the initial conclusion that there is a high level of potential for in-service training leadership within the supervisory ranks of the particular public child welfare agency employed in this project. Although a wide range of apparent initial readiness and ability to assume the training role was found, most supervisors willingly followed the full training trajectory (even role play, modeling, and coaching exercises), understood the nuances of teaching methodology as presented and discussed, displayed increased ability as training progressed and cumulative learning occurred, and indicated that the training had been a particularly beneficial use of the agency's time and other resources.

This experience led to the general conclusion that video-assisted materials and methods such as those in the Vantage Point series may also have particular utility for the preparation of supervisors to assume the direct practice teaching role in agencies serving specific fields of practice other than child protective services.[11] Other recent experiments in using the Vantage Point system in staff development in various settings--mental health (outpatient and in-patient), school social work, corrections, nursing education, mental retardation, public assistance, and family counseling--served to reinforce this conclusion.

On Teaching Old Dogs New Tricks

Experience has reinforced the primary assumption that guides the Vantage Point series--case service supervisors are capable, by and large, of being effective teachers of direct service skill, technique, attitude and values. The tentative conclusion is that though specific training for this important role would be imperative, most supervisors can draw upon vast reserves of experience, resourcefulness, and capability that will surely heighten their changes of success. In fact, Vantage Point staff have witnessed many instances of beautifully effective, impromptu training leadership by supervisors; there are some very good stand-up teachers in the supervisory ranks--some whose ability in this regard came as a rather pleasant surprise to both themselves and agency administrators. It would seem logical for the social service community to inspect seriously the feasibility of "going with its strong suit," and reinforce the ability and opportunity of the supervisor as teacher.

But, of course, this, like any other staff development strategy, has its attendant cost. Opportunities for regular supervisor educational leave, continuing education, and/or contract training workshops would be desirable. Two areas of focus (both of which could be provided by outside educational sources) would be: (1) teaching supervisors in casework process, skills and technique and in relevant theories of human growth and behavior and (2) teaching supervisors to teach this content to their caseworkers or counselors. The supervisors can then employ this knowledge in terms of the unique service nuances of their agency.

One additional point must be made. All will go for naught if the agency administration does not make it possible for regular, systematic teaching of staff by supervisors to take place. This will require precise administrative planning, and scheduling, as well as a way to monitor progress.

The returns are still out on the Tennessee experience. Scattered informal reports indicate the beginning of a wide variance within the Tennessee Department of Human Services in terms of establishing a program of supervisory development of direct service staff, using the Vantage Point materials and methodology. Some supervisors have used the materials extensively and well. Others have not used them at all. New supervisors may or may not be aware of their potential. Other states are beginning to make use of the series, but little is known of their experience to date.

But the proof, as always, is in the pudding. The ingredients are present—materials, methods, supervisors willing to teach, workers willing to learn. Time will tell how well these elements are meshed and coordinated. And that factor, is largely in the hands of agency administration.[12]

FOOTNOTES

1. Christina Maslach, "Burned-Out," Human Behavior, September 1976,
pp. 17-21. Maslach is among those recently involved in the study of this
complex phenomenon in which an emotional distance occurs between the helping
professional and the client or patient. Maslach is particularly interested
in organizational strategies designed to aid professionals to cope with this
ever present danger in the field of human services delivery.

2. Alfred Kadushin, Supervision in Social Work (New York: Columbia
University Press, 1976). Kadushin perhaps has best described the supervisory
training role in contrast to the other roles of management and emotional
support. This book should be considered "must" reading for the social service
supervisor.

3. Armand Lauffer, The Practice of Continuing Education in the Human Services
(New York: McGraw-Hill, 1977), provides a particularly useful resource through
which to examine the diverse patterns and practices in the field of continuing
education. See also Eunice Shatz and Louise Frey, "Principles and Application of the Cooperative Model in Continuing Education," Journal of Education
for Social Work, Vol. 13, No. 3 (Fall 1977), pp. 91-98, in reference to
cooperative agency ventures. Of further interest to the reader may be
Kenneth Krause, "Interagency Training: A Cooperative Approach to Staff
Development," Child Welfare, Vol. 56, No. 6 (June 1977), pp. 361-367.

4. The theme of the necessity of providing training of immediate utilitarian
value, tailored to local conditions and needs, recurs often in the literature. One such recent reiteration may be found in "Training Issues and Needs,"
in Proceedings of the First National Conference on Child Abuse and Neglect,
DHEW Publication Number (OHD) 77-30094, Workshop A2, pp. 81-82.

5. Thomas Cruthirds, Marcia Roe and Don Wilson, "Final Report and
Evaluation of Tennessee Child Protection Training Project," Urban Observatory
of Metropolitan Nashville - University Centers, unpublished mimeographed
report, January 1976, p. 2.

6. See Thomas Cruthirds, "Project Proposal for Development and Utilization
of Videotape Training Materials in the Public Social Services," unpublished
mimoegraphed proposal, The University of Tennessee School of Social Work,
May 1976.

7. Aaron Krasner, in "The Development and Use of Video Stimulus Tapes
for Training Social Work Field Instructors," a paper presented at the Annual
Program Meeting of the Council on Social Work Education, 1975, seems to have
coined this very descriptive phrase.

8. Phillip Popple, Thomas Cruthirds, David Kurtz and Robert Williams,
A Training Guide on Working with Parents Who Neglect Their Children
(Knoxville: The University of Tennessee Research Corporation, 1977).

9. Thomas Cruthirds, Beth Parrish and Sue Gerrity, A Training Guide on
Working with Children in Day Care (Knoxville: The University of Tennessee
Research Corporation, 1977).

10. Information on these materials is available from The University of Tennessee Research Corporation, 404 Andy Holt Tower, Knoxville, Tennessee, 37916.

11. Bonnie C. Rhim, "The Use of Videotapes In Social Work Agencies," Social Casework (December 1976), pp. 644-650, is one of several recent contributions to this growing body of experience and knowledge. And of course the seminal work in this field is highly recommended reading, Ida Oswald and Suzanne Wilson, This Bag Is Not A Toy: A Handbook for The Use of Video-recording in Educating for the Professions (New York: Council on Social Work Education, 1971).

12. For the author's view on the responsibilities of agency management to properly "serve" the technical core of caseworkers and first-line supervisors see, Thomas Cruthirds, "Management Should Be Accountable, Too," Comments on Currents, Social Work, Vol. 21, No. 3 (May 1976), pp. 179-180.

Training for Evaluation:
Fact or Fiction?

by Patricia Drew and Ernest Kahn

Patricia Drew, D.S.W., is Associate Professor and Director of the Research Center at the University of Maryland at Baltimore School of Social Work and Community Planning. Ernest Kahn, Ph.D., is Associate Professor and Assistant Dean at the University of Maryland School of Social Work and Community Planning.

During the 1976-1977 academic year, the authors, together with project staff, engaged in a project entitled "Title XX Child Welfare Programs: Evaluation Training Model Development," under a grant from the Public Services Administration of DHEW.[1] The principal objective of the project was the development of curriculum materials for training in evaluation. Data concerning needs and issues in evaluation training were gathered through several approaches from a large number of sources. Among these were a mail survey of evaluation training activities and plans in the public welfare services of all of the states and an intensive on-site examination by project staff of incentives and constraints concerning evaluation in an eight state sample. In addition, three regional meetings were conducted and attended by 120 key staff members of public social service systems in 42 states which served both to further assess needs and to provide initial opportunities to test curriculum modules.

The conference participants were staff members with responsibilities for administration, evaluation or staff development. The reasons for the inclusion of personnel with administrative and evaluative responsibilities must be self-evident. Staff developers/trainers were involved because of their particular responsibilities for addressing the training of staff engaged in direct service delivery and/or supervisory assignments.

The data from the various sources converged to reveal issues in training for evaluation which recurred frequently within the three staff groupings.

Issues in Training for Evaluation

Training issues were identified for the three functional groups. For administrators the issues were: (1) understanding regulations regarding Title XX reporting and requirements for evaluation; (2) developing and utilizing management information systems; (3) decision making for program evaluation; (4) understanding evaluation models, methods and techniques; and (5) opening communication lines with evaluation and training personnel.

For evaluators, training issues were: (1) planning for evaluation; (2) determining data needed for evaluation; (3) developing models for needs assessment, planning, decision making, program evaluation, monitoring, data collection and feedback; (4) opening communication lines with administrative and training staff; (5) coping with demands for immediate, relevant evaluative data for decision making; (6) establishing criteria of effect, especially outcome measures; (7) sampling strategies; (8) conducting field studies; and (9) using computer data for evaluation.

The issues for staff developers/trainers were: (1) how to train evaluators in service delivery programs; (2) how to train staff in service and purchase-of-service contracts in evaluation, including data collection; (3) how to motivate staff to overcome apathy and resistance towards evaluation; (4) how to interpret the significance of evaluation training when program evaluation competes with service monies; (5) how to open communication with administrative and evaluation staff; (6) how to clarify the differences between monitoring and evaluation; (7) how to enable line staff to become an integral part of proper evaluation—planning and implementation; and (8) how to assess evaluation training needs and evaluate such training when offered.

Training Principles

Principles, which represented a base for our development of training curricula, were derived from these issues. These principles are:

1. All levels of staff of a social service system need training in order to participate appropriately in program evaluation.

2. The training of the various levels of staff should be on a "need to know" basis; i.e., all staff members do not need to know all of the same content.

3. Evaluation is an integral part of administrative decision making.

4. Staff development personnel need to be involved in the administrative processes prior to any decision to undertake evaluation activities.

5. There is a need for clarity regarding roles and functions of administrators, evaluators, and line and staff development personnel with regard to program evaluation.

6. The lack of a single model of evaluation precludes the development of a singular model of training for evaluation.

7. The diversity in the utilization of the several existing models of evaluation requires further adaptation by any one system of the materials for training in evaluation.

Our curricula materials are grounded in these principles. We would like to expand briefly upon them to assist in understanding the focus and the thrust of the curricula.

The first principle of training for evaluation for all levels of staff cannot be emphasized enough. While the statement is simple and perhaps even readily acceptable, it may mislead in its simplicity or unintentionally obscure some ramifications. The range of need for training extends literally from the chief administrator of the system to all staff members engaged in direct service delivery. A program administrator needs to have very clear recognition of what program evaluation and evaluative research can and cannot do for his organization. He needs to be able to understand the kinds of issues with which evaluation research can and may deal; the approaches to such issues; the scope, depth and time frame involved in evaluation research; and so forth.

Other echelons of the service system have training needs related to the scope of authority and function of the particular person. As one moves lower in the echelons of any one service system, it is likely that the range of issues will narrow considerably. It is also possible to identify a shift in emphasis which any of the issues may have for staff at lower levels.

Few, if any, states are likely to have personnel available which can focus solely on the collection of data for evaluation research. It seems inevitable, therefore, that the basic data will need to be collected by the "front-line" staff of any department, i.e., the direct service workers who come in day-by-day contact with the clients of the system. We recognize that there is an entire set of issues which speaks directly to the impact which evaluation may have on relationships between workers and clients and on the methods of service delivery. At the moment, however, we are concerned with stressing that direct service workers are not only in need of training but particularly in need of it, because so much of any evaluation effort depends on the accuracy of the data which they compile. Frequently, serious reservations are expressed about the accuracy of data which are obtained by evaluators from direct service workers, even when data collection devices are well thought out and prepared. The various constraints and numerous concerns of service workers regarding the submission of such evaluation data simply increases the need for appropriate training for this level of staff.

Various members of middle management, such as supervisory staff, should be knowledgeable about evaluation to the extent that they can both provide necessary assistance and support to members of their staff and recognize the various ways in which evaluation can assist or possibly constrain the activities of their program.

Further, the various echelons of support staff of a statewide system are also in need of such training. We will discuss the crucial roles of evaluators and staff developers later. However, it is essential that personnel engaged in legislative liaison and public relations understand the potential and limitations of evaluation.

A significant difference arises in the type of knowledge that is required. We are suggesting that every staff member does not need to know the same about program evaluation.

Program evaluation is an essential instrument of administrative decision making with distinct and definable uses in the review, reorganization, or even reconceptualization of service programs. As such, it is an administrative approach which focuses on the establishment of foundations for changes in service delivery systems in accordance with other changes taking place in the population to be served, the environment in which the service system is functioning, or the mission of the service organization itself. Program evaluation also can demonstrate program effectiveness, therefore, confirming the validity of on-going programs.

Such an administrative approach has important benefits for the acceptance and utilization of program evaluation in a public social system which endeavors to be self-corrective. It conveys to the members of the system a clear understanding that expectations and requirements for evaluation are to be met with the same seriousness as holds true for other administrative requirements. Failure on the part of staff to respond accordingly can be expected to have negative consequences. Integrally linked with this is the right of staff to expect appropriate explanations concerning the objectives of program evaluation; the methods and procedures to be used in the implementation of such a program; the use to which findings will be put and appropriate reassurance concerning the safeguards of the rights of both clients and staff members. Especially important is the need to feed back the results of program evaluation to staff members so that they can utilize the findings for a review of their own activities and possible changes of these.

For the human services administrator, the conceptualization of evaluation as a specific segment of decision making also can hold important benefits vis-a-vis the agency's sanctioning sources. A system which seeks to engage in regular evaluation of its activities and endeavors to implement changes on the basis of the results should be able to secure more adequate resources for such efforts and a degree of tolerance for time to utilize the evaluation findings.

This position, in turn, raises several significant training issues. As previously stated, there is no one accepted standard model of program evaluation. There is need in the case of program evaluation first to determine the type of evaluation which is to be conducted. It is likely that no one model of evaluation will prove satisfactory for all of the needs of a large public social service system. Important decisions should be made about the appropriate evaluation strategy given the purpose of the evaluation.

This current condition presents the human services administrator with a rather unique situation. It requires that the administrator and his key aides will be required to obtain a thorough grounding in program evaluation prior to any decisions concerning its use and implementation in the program. Failure to do so will result in an almost assured set of difficulties as the evaluation effort itself is undertaken.

Trainers in the public social services may have to deal with staff reluctance to move rapidly with technological innovation and with the potentially more serious reluctance of upper echelon managers to engage in conceptual rather than problem solving approaches to the management of public social service programs.

It is hoped that at some point after the understanding suggested has been obtained, a service system will move to employ members of an evaluation staff. In our project, we made an assumption at the outset which did not prove to be true. Specifically, we assumed that evaluators currently employed in the public social services would have competence in program evaluation methodology but possibly would know little, if anything, about the history, purposes and services of the programs. Instead, we found that in a substantial number of states, the personnel assigned to program evaluation did not have specific education or experience in this field of endeavor.

The ramifications of this state of affairs are almost too obvious to require any comment. Coupled with an apparent reluctance of administrators to obtain a basic grounding in evaluation concepts, the lack of expertise on the part of the staff specifically assigned to evaluation raises the most serious possible questions concerning any success of such efforts and has direct import for learning.

The curriculum which we have developed assigns a role of critical importance to the staff development personnel of the agencies. Essentially, it becomes their responsibility to develop and deliver the training activities which will address the varied deficits suggested in the discussion of the other principles. It is not the responsibility of staff developers to become expert themselves in evaluation methodology. The precedent of calling on outside resources to meet specific needs, a practice established by staff development divisions, can well be utilized in evaluation. However, as in other areas of work, the staff developers should be responsible for the relevance and applicability of the training for the work in which the particular trainees are engaged. In the case of program evaluation, this implies a prior understanding of the extent to which the trainees need to know and will be expected to participate in evaluation.

Staff developers, as the employers of outside experts, should have a clear understanding of the particular evaluation model to be utilized in any one program and the evaluation goals which the model is expected to meet. Staff developers need not be evaluation experts but they do need the expertise to evaluate the appropriateness of the material and the competence of the outside expert who is to do the training. It is perhaps saying the obvious when one adds that staff developers will therefore need an understanding of the basics of program evaluation including its various models and the types of evaluations which the organization can implement.

In training for evaluation in large organizations, staff developers should take a strongly proactive stand and be involved in the process of implementing an evaluation system from the very beginning. Ideally, they should be involved as early as the provision of the basic background in evaluation which we have suggested as essential for the executive of the service system and his key deputies. Staff developers certainly need to be involved when consideration is given to a choice of evaluation models to be utilized by a system. Not only do the models vary significantly but they address different issues and produce different levels of results. Accordingly, they require training on different levels of complexity and create different sets of demands on time and other resources as well as differential concerns about their implications for clients and staff members. The proactive staff developer should certainly be able, and in turn be enabled by the leadership of the organization, to assess these concerns and to have them considered among the factors which influence the choice of the model of evaluation which the agency will use.

In view of what has already been said about the diversity of programs throughout the country, it seems hardly necessary to detail the reasons which require curriculum modules that will still require further local adaptation. Diversity exists in so many different areas--agency structure, auspices, financing, programs, departmental priorities, and others--that it would be thoroughly misleading to suggest that any one module could be "plugged in" without further review and tailoring to specific needs. Just as there is no one model of evaluation, there can be no model of training for evaluation!

What we have attempted to define is what the various members of a public social service system need to know in order for that system to engage in program evaluation efforts. We did so by developing three curriculum segments. These training curricula are:

1. A course in evaluation research.

2. An administrative model of program evaluation.

3. A staff development training package.

Evaluation Research

The course on evaluation research is designed in modules so that segments of it can be utilized for personnel with different functions and different staff development needs related to evaluation. It was thought that program staff might need an overview of evaluation, as well as instruction in selecting valid reliable criteria of effect and generating accurate data. Administrators may wish to consider evaluation foci or the systems implications of various evaluation research designs. Evaluators, on the other hand, should consider the appropriateness of various evaluation research models, given various evaluation objectives and the nature of the program to be evaluated. Each module in the course lists the topics to be covered and the content of the module, and presents a suggested bibliography.

The course assumes a background in research, i.e., knowledge of and/or experience in the application of the scientific method. For staff members who lack such a background, a prerequisite course would be an introduction to research and the curricula which we have prepared.

The course in evaluation research addresses itself to the following areas:

1. _Program Assessment_. The topics to be covered in this module include accountability, evaluation research and monitoring, and decision

making. The last of these addresses the need to know both from the perspective of evaluation research as a management tool and from the relationship of evaluation research to social policy.

2. <u>Purposes and Categories of Evaluation</u>. This module includes the following topics: reasons for evaluation; decision making typologies; and evaluation research categories. Particular attention is given to the typologies for decision making since, as we have already discussed, we view evaluation as an important resource for the administrator in engaging in this process.

3. <u>Evaluation Research Models</u>. This module discusses evaluation models which are potentially available for use in the public social services. The models covered include goal attainment, the system model, the impact model, cost benefit analysis, planning programming budgetary systems (PPBS), and the service input/output/outcome model. Each of these models is discussed in concise terms which specify what the particular model can be expected to achieve. Each model is depicted in detail including the use of flow charts.

4. <u>The Evaluation Planning Process</u>. This module is one which will be of particular interest to those more directly engaged in evaluation, including both the evaluation staff itself and those administrators responsible for policy decisions regarding evaluation. Among the topics to be considered in the module are the choice of an appropriate model of evaluation given the evaluation objective; the data required with special attention to the originators of the request, the consumers of the end product as well as the purpose of the evaluation and its time frame. The nature of the program is a further segment of this particular module. This module also contains a number of chart presentations which could, if desired, readily be utilized as visual aid materials.

5. Evaluation Research Methodology. This module will presumably be of particular interest to people who are closely involved with the program evaluation efforts of the service system. The topics covered in the module include: comparative analysis; experimental, quasi-experimental and pre-experimental design; criteria of effect; and both internal and external validity. The various designs are specifically presented as are the factors which make for internal or external validity of an evaluation research design. In addition to validity, there is also a discussion of reliability.

6. The Relationship of Evaluation Research to Agency Operation. The module addresses itself both to the conduct of an evaluation effort and to the politics of evaluation. It deals with considerations which go far beyond the technical concerns of evaluation staff and impact on many levels of staff in a number of different ways. The issues raised are intended both to stimulate discussion as well as to suggest possible approaches. This module is also a good example of critical issues in evaluation research for which no definite answers can be given. The curriculum considers such factors prior to the initiation and implementation of evaluation so that strategies can be developed to deal with such concerns on either an operational or a contingency basis.

7. Utilization of Evaluation Research. The module concerns itself with the qualities of "good" research from the perspectives of both the administrative decision maker and the academic researcher. The various elements are listed and available for detailed analyses. The module also contains a discussion of the implications of the "era of accountability" for social service programs. Other issues considered in the module include the need for the identification of dissatisfactions and concerns prior to the initiation of evaluation; the need to articulate reasons for evaluation;

the timing of evaluation efforts; and the circumstances for informal evaluation.

The introductory research course for staff members who do not have such knowledge considers scientific problem forumulation including theory construction, ethics of research, and problem formulation. It contains a major unit on research methodology which covers basic considerations of sampling, design, hypothesis testing, and data collection. Among other topics included in this introductory course are instrument construction; classification and table construction; descriptive and inferential statistical tools for data analysis; research report writing and the state of knowledge in social work research.

While this introductory course is intended for "make-up work" by staff not familiar with the concepts, the modules of the primary course are intended to supply the fundamental knowledge about evaluation research required by various levels and units of staff in the public social services. This one course and its seven modules obviously do not cover all the knowledge in evaluation research and some members of the service delivery organization, among them, most certainly, the evaluation staff itself, will need to secure such specialized knowledge from other sources, e.g., schools of social work and other graduate programs.

Program Evaluation

We have already stated that our approach to the training for evaluation is grounded in, among other principles, the conviction that evaluation represents an increasingly significant tool for administrative decision-making. Therfore, the second major component of the materials which have been prepared depicts an administrative model of program evaluation. It offers both a discussion of the significant considerations involved in this approach and a course outline which specifies topics to be covered. It outlines assignments for participants and gives a bibliography for further reading. The topics covered in the proposed training curriculum include the following:

1. The social, political and economic context of program evaluation.

2. Analytical perspectives on organizational or program performance.

3. Program evaluation as a management function.

4. Program evaluation and the problem of values.

5. Management techniques related to program evaluation.

The fifth topic addresses itself to four different management techniques and includes management information system (MIS); management by objectives (MBO); program planning and budgeting systems (PPBS); and zero-based budgeting (ZBB).

Unlike the curriculum material described previously, this course is not intended to serve as a research course. Instead, its primary focus is on the administrator's responsibility for establishing arrangements whereby program performance can be judged along previously established dimensions. The outline also specifies knowledge, skill and attitude objectives.

The curriculum materials reflect the contemporary and increasing expectations for accountability and the particular manner in which these have developed in the field of social welfare. These are contrasted to the underlying assumptions of program evaluation itself and a conceptual framework is developed which reflects the location of social welfare programs within formal organizations. The perspective is one based on the "open system" concept and also reflects the cyclical view of organizational performance which this systems perspective maintains. The material:

...calls particular attention to three critical administrative tasks in connection with program performance around which program evaluation must revolve: (1) the acquisition of sufficient resources, including clients to insure not only the expected performance, but also the survival of the organizational program; (2) the conduct of the program and the delivery of its services with maximum efficiency; and (3) the relationship of "means" to "ends" in terms of goal achievement, i.e., the demonstration of program effectiveness (or ineffectiveness).[2]

Another important linkage between administrative decision making and program evaluation is suggested in the need for the establishment and maintenance of a monitoring or management information system "...designed to provide comprehensive data which will enable the administrator and the program evaluator to assertain the extent to which the program is successfully executing the tasks specified...and the extent to which the program may be considered to be of value."[3]

Staff Developers' Training Package

The third major segment of the curricula materials developed through this project contrasts sharply with the approach just described for the first two courses. While these courses contain modular content which allows for their adaptation to the needs of the various service systems, the third segment represents an entire training package. It is intended as a staff development training package and addresses itself to the ways in which staff developers go about the planning, designing, implementation and evaluation of training for evaluation in public social service delivery systems. It is based directly on input received by the project staff from staff development directors who participated in the project's three regional conferences. At these sessions the staff development directors identified a number of broad issues and the resultant curriculum modules attempt to deal with the most common and pressing issues faced by staff development divisions in training for evaluation.

The issues emerged from a simple schematic approach in which state staff development directors were asked the following:

> Assuming your state wants to evaluate and your primary role as a staff development director is to design training for this evaluation effort, what do you need to know and what skills do you need in order to fulfill your role?

The responses to this question generated a number of staff development issues which were structured into five broad training areas. A training module was developed for each of these as follows:

1. Understanding the evaluation process.

2. Understanding evaluation in complex systems.

3. Understanding the role of the staff deelopment in the evaluation process.

4. Planning for training for evaluation.

5. Designing training for evaluation.

The five modules form a complete training package in the basics of training for evaluation. Each single module is related to the other four; however, each module may also stand alone.

For each of the five modules we have indicated the total length of time as well as the specific time for each of the specified learning objectives. Teaching content and teaching points are indicated together with the preferred instructional method for each point. Appropriate readings are also specified and will be supplied with the modules themselves. The first of these modules is intended as a basic program to familiarize nonevaluation personnel with the overall process of evaluation. It is projected for two days of training (12 instructional hours). The second module is planned for one training day, while the third, fourth and fifth units also require two training days each.

An Evaluation Training Model

This training model is based on the position that when a decision is made to evaluate, there are three primary units that ideally will work together in mounting and maintaining the evaluation effort. Policy makers and program administrators have the initial responsibility for deciding to mount an evaluation effort and for providing the impetus to evaluate, the administrative supports necessary and the resources needed for that effort. The importance of administrative commitment and support cannot be overemphasized. Once this occurs, evaluation personnel will begin to work on the planning of the evaluation effort, specifically the methodology. Evaluators have the clear responsibility for the selection and/or design of an appropriate evaluation model that will effect desired results within the limits of the agency's budgetary, personnel and technological parameters. At this point, however, a third group must be involved in the effort. Levels of personnel, operating in a variety of functional areas, will be affected, directly or indirectly, by an agency's evaluation effort. These personnel must know, to varying degrees of complexity and sophistication, the what, why, how, when and where of evaluation. It is at this point in the process that the staff development unit can and should perform a critical function, i.e., the continuous preparation of agency personnel to activate, maintain, and make appropriate use of the agency's evaluation effort. Staff development must use its expertise--training and internal consultation--as tools to effect planned change so that the entire evaluation effort is not sabotaged internally, either directly through lack of knowledge and skills in evaluation, or indirectly, through fear of and resistance to the evaluation effort.

Our project experience revealed problems in mounting and maintaining program evaluation efforts in the public social service delivery system. Some of these problems and issues, we think, exist in the humans services field in general within both the public and private sector. Factors, including the politics, funding and organizational cost-versus-benefit, influence evaluation in an action arena.

In the persepctive of all of these considerations, is training for evaluation then fact or fiction? In seeking an answer, some facts can clearly be established. Among these are: a continuing trend toward accountability; the need for tools to respond to this expectation; the availability of evaluation as an aid to administrative decision making; the variety of approaches to program evaluation.

There is also another set of facts which must be considered in answering this question. Our social service systems employ many dedicated people who know programs and policies but not evaluation methodology. People who do know evaluation research usually are not expert in social service programs. If evaluations of high quality are to be conducted, this dichotomy requires resolution. In our view, the method for its resolution is training.

However, there is still a third set of facts to be weighed in this context. Within the limits of this presentation, we have suggested that evaluation efforts in human services face serious contraints from politics, funding, cost/benefit and other considerations. We do not suggest that training can eliminate, or even ameliorate, such factors. It is indeed entirely possible that, until these factors are resolved by other means, significant evaluation efforts will not be possible.

However, if and when political and funding constraints are resolved, good program evaluations still will not be automatically possible. The

removal of outside obstacles does not give the staff of any organization
the knowledge, skills and particularly the attitudes which are essential
for the conduct of evaluation. To acquire these, training is imperative.
And for that reason, training for evaluation is fact and not fiction. It
is also a necessity and not a luxury.

FOOTNOTES

1. Patricia Drew and Ernest Kahn, <u>Title XX Child Welfare Programs:</u> <u>Evaluation Training Model Development Project Report</u> Two Volumes (Baltimore: University of Maryland School of Social Work and Community Planning, 1977).

2. <u>Ibid.</u>, p. 78.

3. <u>Ibid.</u>

III. The Design of Training Techniques

The authors in Section III focus on the design of Training Techniques.
They provide a more detailed picture of specific techniques used in training
program development. Patricia Dunn provides a model for designing a training
program on training in the human services. Judith Warren and Glenn McKibbin
discuss the need to use a futures orientation or continuous needs assessment
in the development of any training programs. Both Max Casper and Vincent
Faherty discuss the use of simulation approaches as a basic training technique.

Dunn focuses on the techniques of training human service trainers.
She starts by briefly discussing the need for a significant increase in
this activity based on the rapid growth of continuing education efforts in
the field. She then presents a conceptual framework on which such training
should be based. This framework focuses both on what is learned (substance)
and how it is learned (process). The analysis of what is to be learned
includes such tasks as task analysis, component task achievement, intratask
transfer and sequencing. The analysis of how it is to be learned includes
dealing with such principles as motivation, practicing behaviors, training
design, modeling and training climate.

She then proposes a model technique for developing a training in training program. The following areas are discussed: selection and assessment of participants; establishing training goals and objectives; development of training design; selection of trainers; establishment of training climate and evaluation of the program.

Warren and McKibbin present an approach to training program development which involves the technique of ongoing needs assessment throughout the training process. They call this futures orientation to training program planning. The use of this technique in the development of a consumer education training program for older adults is discussed.

They argue that using a futures orientation ensures that trainers will actually use the training once they have returned to work. They call for a focus on alternative future implementation during the planning process, which would include identification of the critical factors influencing implementation. They urge analysis of such factors as the characteristics of the macro-sociopolitical unit, the characteristics of the organization itself and the characteristics of the trainees. They describe how this technique was used in the consumer education program.

Both Casper and Faherty discuss the use of the technique of simulation as a training approach. Casper describes the development and use of SIMSWRK (Simulated Social Work), a simulation approach used at Syracuse to orient incoming social work students to the gestalt of social work intervention in community, agency and family life. The rationale for this technique is presented and a detailed design of SIMSWRK is provided. An assessment of the use of this technique is discussed, based on its actual use at Syracuse with suggestions as to how it can be most effectively utilized in social work training.

Faherty presents the use of SIMSI (Simulation of Services Integration), a simulating technique aimed at giving human service providers an awareness of the complexities of human services integration, an understanding of two disparate approaches to integration and an appreciation of how to use the best approach.

He discusses the validity of using simulation as a training technique, presents the SIMSI technique in detail and provides an assessment of the experience in using this approach and how it can best be used by others.

A Model for Training Beginning Trainers

by Patricia C. Dunn

Patricia C. Dunn, M.S.W., is Assistant Professor with the Continuing Education Program at Rutgers University Graduate School of Social Work.

The purpose of this paper is to present a model for training human service delivery professionals who have training and teaching responsibilities. The model is based on a conceptual framework which is operationalized in a Basic Training for Trainers program. The program is guided by general principles relating to what is learned—the program's goals and objectives, and how it is learned—the conditions under which objectives are achieved. Evaluation is considered an integral and continuing component of the program. I shall discuss the need for training human service continuing education specialists, define the conceptual base for the training model and describe the model itself.

THE NEED

In a major study of continuing education in Schools of Social Work, Phyllis Southwick made nine recommendations to continuing education directors.[1] Among them was the suggestion that programs be implemented which train continuing education specialists to teach the adult learner. Southwick's edict is timely since social service delivery personnel are being called upon, at an alarming rate, to train fellow practitioners, and professional schools are being asked to develop continuing education programs to meet the requirements of ever expanding fields of knowledge as well as the demands of licensure and recertification. Lois Swack notes that "no branch of the professional education system is growing faster than continuing education."[2] Yet social workers and kindred professionals have little opportunity to develop the necessary skills for training others.

There are two prevalent "folk" assumptions concerning training: one, that a good "doer" (practitioner) should be able to teach others to do; the other, that training is an art best practiced by those with "native ability." Like most folklore, these assumptions have some base in reality. Training effectiveness, however, depends more on acquired skills and the application of these skills in a multiplicity of situational and organizational settings than on native ability. Given the trend of increasing continuing education demands and a lack of skilled teachers of professionals adults to meet these demands, training for trainers becomes an imperative.

CONCEPTUAL FRAMEWORK

While no systematic conceptual framework exists in the learning and training literature, a variety of learning assumptions and concepts have been designated as guides to designing and implementing effective training programs. In the construction of our model for training trainers, these general principles have been useful. They fall into two categories: what is learned and how it is learned. The what consists of analyzing and arranging subject matter.[3] The how includes selecting and sequencing media to facilitate the creation and maintenance of a supportive learning climate.[4]

What Is Learned--The Training Goals

Robert Gagné suggests that primary consideration should be given to what is learned.[5] The principles involved in his formulations and utilized in the model are: task analysis, component task achievement, intratask transfer, and sequencing.

Task analysis suggests a method for identifying the component tasks or a terminal task or a final performance. In other words, the final performance trainer may be broken down into a hierarchy of components or subtasks. Task hierarchies may be based upon: (1) complexity, in which the hierarchy proceeds from least to most complex; (2) sequence, with the hierarchy ranging from what to do first to what to do last in terms of learning efficiency; and (3) prerequisites, in which the hierarchy goes from the first skill to be acquired to terminal behaviors.[6] Hierarchies based upon sequence prerequisites are most applicable in the Basic Training for Trainers Model.

Component task achievement concerns the achievement of subtasks which are mediators of the final task performance.[7] The achievement of component tasks ensures intratask transfer.

Intratask transfer is a process in which the achievement of mediating tasks ensures positive transfer to the final performance, while their absence reduces such transfer to near zero. In other words, in order to assure arrival at a goal, certain subgoals must be accomplished. Without the accomplishment of the subgoals, final goal accomplishment becomes almost impossible.

Sequencing is the final process. Component tasks, based on their hierarchical relationship to each other and the final task performance, are sequenced. According to Gagné, sequencing involves arranging the total training situation in an order that will ensure optimal mediational effects from one component task to another and finally to the terminal task performance.[8] In this model, the sequencing of the program units which correspond with what Gagné calls tasks, is based on hierarchies of efficiency and prerequisites.

How It Is Learned--The Training Process

The second category of theoretical concepts concerns the learning process. The key factors governing the learning process include motivation, practice, modeling, training design and training climate.

__Motivation__ refers to "forces" which cause the participant to approach training actively and with interest. The trainee exhibits "approach responses" rather than "avoidance responses" to the goals and objectives of the program. The participants want to learn what is being taught. Campbell, et al., note that motivation is enhanced by voluntary enrollment in the program and the opportunity to participate in modifying program objectives to meet personal needs.[9]

__Practice__ of the learned behavior is viewed by Gagné and Campbell as essential to task accomplishment, i.e., the participant must not only "learn" the behavior, but must practice it. However, practice alone is not sufficient; it is practice with feedback that results in optimal learning. Feedback, or the knowledge of results, enhances learning in two ways: it allows the participant to correct mistakes and it makes the learning task more intrinsically rewarding or interesting. It is especially effective if it comes soon after the learner's response and indicates the appropriateness of the response so it can be reinforced or corrected. In addition, spaced learning or practice periods have been shown to be more effective for learning than "massed practice".[11] Hence training for trainers programs, especially those geared for beginning trainers, should be "spaced" over several months.

Training design, in general, is concerned with the presentation of responses to be learned in an organized fashion via some kind of coded and symbolic means.[12] In other words, designing is the ordering of media (lectures, group discussion, structural tasks, simulations, etc.) to accomplish training goals and objectives. The utilization of particular media also influences the learning climate in terms of quality of participant involvement.

Modeling involves learning by the participant imitating the behaviors of the trainers. The attraction of the model and factors which influence the model's relationship to the participant are important. As with the training design, a key aspect mediating the attraction and the relationship is the training climate.

Training climate, as defined by Rolf Lynton and Udai Pareek[13] and Ned Flanders,[14] is the affective component of learning. Feelings about the learning process can block or enhance the rate of progress toward training goals accomplishment. If the learning climate is defensive, it becomes very difficult for things to go right.

THE MODEL

    Selection and Assessment of Participants

    Training Goals and Objectives

    Training Design

    Trainers

Training Climate

Evaluation

Selection and Assessment of Participants

It is important to establish criteria for selecting participants, since the type of training programs this model represents not only knowledge about training but also practice in using training skills. The number of participants should be restricted according to the number of trainers for the skill practice sessions. In our programs we have found that a seven-to-one ratio works well. A brochure containing the description, the goals and objectives of the program, and an application designed to facilitate the selection process should be disseminated. Applicants may be selected according to the following criteria: (1) currently training or will be training in the immediate future; (2) have an area of expertise; and (3) have their employer's permission to attend the program without missing sessions due to work responsibilities. Telephone interviews may be used to augment the selection process.

Once the participants are selected, an assessment of each person's needs should begin. In our programs we, in addition to making use of the information on the application forms and the results of any interviews, administer a questionnaire to each participant prior to the first session. The questionnaire is keyed to specific objectives of the program and is designed to provide reliable indications of the particular needs of the participants. It also serves as a pretest and posttest for the program's evaluation process. Additional information is solicited during the first session, providing participants with further opportunity to express their learning needs.

Training Goals and Objectives

To identify what is to be taught in order to produce a trainer, learning and training literature was analyzed and experienced trainers in universities, industry and human service delivery systems were interviewed. Via this process we identified seven subtasks of the task trainer which became the goals of the program.[15] The goals, as written for the participants, are as follows:

1. Be able to understand the role of the trainer in an organization.
2. Be able to analyze the training needs of organizations and individuals.
3. Be able to select goals and write performance objectives.
4. Be able to evaluate the effectiveness of training outcome.
5. Be able to design training programs.
6. Be able to create supportive learning climates.
7. Be able to implement training programs.

The goals are sequenced according to a learning hierarchy based on our perception of the most efficient method and order for teaching. This arrangement insures positive transfer from skills of lower position to connected ones of higher position. The terminal task of the trainer requires the acquisition of the seven identified subtasks which are mediators of the task trainer. To be operationalized the goals are defined as performance objectives which state specifically what the participant will be able to do to demonstrate goal acquisition. The performance objectives alter with each participant cohort as they not only define the goal but reflect participant needs.

The program trainers take primary responsibility for writing the performance objectives, although participants have input based on their needs. The objectives serve as a contract between the trainers and participants and are renegotiated as necessary. The hierarchical sequence of goals and objectives is implemented as a learning design in which media are selected and ordered to meet training objectives and to facilitate the creation of a supportive learning climate.

The Training Design

Campbell states that the training design in general is concerned with the presentation of responses to be learned in an organized fashion via some kind of coded or symbolic means.[16] In other phraseology, it is the process of selecting the ordering media to accomplish training goals and objectives. Media range from abstract to concrete. Malcolm Knowles defines abstract devices as books, chalkboards, lectures, maps, filmstrips and other similar devices which primarily engage the senses of sight and hearing.[17] Concrete devices involve doing as well as seeing and hearing, and include simulations, structured tasks, games, skill practice sessions and video tape practice sessions. Since a major concern of this model is to provide participants with experiences that maximize intratask transfer and training transfer to the work setting, emphasis is on concrete experiences which are more efficient for making learning transfer possible.

There are four procedures which we use throughout the program: (1) the provision of practice opportunities under controlled circumstances; (2) the provision of all required materials and texts to eliminate stress and time pressures faced by busy practitioners who must search for the required materials; (3) the establishment of a resource library within the training room for participant use (materials participants have found helpful are shared with others); and (4) the utilization of precourse and other outside assignments to maximize the learning experience and reduce the use of the lecture method.

Spaced sessions are also an important aspect of the training design. Spacing the sessions enables the participants to integrate concepts, practice skills, experiment on the job, and receive feedback from the program trainers.

The Trainers

The training team approach is most effective as it offers divergent points of view, a wide range of trainer perceptions, more than one model for emulation, and opportunities for participants to receive individualized attention and skill practice. Team balance is important. Teaching styles, experience in management, experience in direct service, professional discipline, and previous teaching/training experience are all factors to be considered when building a training team.

The team's modeling function is one of the most important aspects of this type of training. The attraction of the model and factors which influence the model's relationship to the participant are important. The key aspect mediating the attraction is the training climate.

Training Climate

The environment of the training session can stimulate or block the learning experiences of the participants. Therefore, careful consideration must be given to both the physical and psychological aspects of the training climate. The physical aspects of training such as room size, temperature, seating arrangements, name tags, coffee, parking instructions, length of sessions, time of day, must be given attention. Concomitantly, the trainers must share the responsibility of program output with the participants, express concern about their problems, demonstrate that they are valued as people, encourage the participants in formulation of the program's performance objectives so that the objectives are in line with their needs. The trainers are the major influence on the climate of a training session. When the trainers' behaviors are directed toward the establishment of supportive learning climate, the participants feel free to express their concerns and generally are accepting of new tasks and ideas.

Evaluation

Evaluation is an integral component of this model. The evaluative focus is on the achievement of program objectives (what is learned) and program process (how it is learned).

Program objectives can be measured by the utilization of an objective instrument and the evaluation of participant products such as written training designs and videotapes of practice sessions. An objective instrument has been constructed which focuses on three of the program's goal areas: (1) trainer role, (2) analysis of the need for training, and (3) performance objectives. The instrument contains the following:

GOAL	TEST ITEM
Trainer Role	Sixteen items describe various organizational behaviors. The respondent indicates which behaviors agree with trainer role.
Analysis of Training Needs	Fifteen vignettes involve training requests by agency administrators. The respondent indicates which requests involve skill decisions and thus make training appropriate.
Performance Objectives	Forty training objectives are listed. The respondent indicates which objectives meet the criteria of performance objectives.

To validate the instrument, two program trainers completed it. Any question upon which there was disagreement was excluded. The reliability of the instrument was established by the split-half technique. The coefficient of reliability was +.96.

For the first few times that a course based on the models is offered, the design for evaluating the achievement of program objectives should involve a comparison between the scores of the participant group and a control or comparison group on the objective instrument in a pretest/post-test format. The control group should be selected in terms of its equivalence to the participant group. If a control group cannot be obtained or if, as has been our experience, control groups have been used in the past but are no longer used because of economic factors, the group could become its own control. The design would consist of measuring again at the very beginning of the training but before training input influence, and then a third measure after training input. The time intervals between measurements should be comparable. If the changes between measurements two and three are greater than those between one and two, then the inference is that training has caused these changes.[18]

Thus far the focus has been on collecting data with respect to what is learned. Evaluation of most training has been largely neglected in this area, placing more emphasis on how participants feel about the learning experience. Feelings about learning experiences must be considered. However, how the participants felt about the learning experience is of no greater importance in the evaluation process than what they learned. Form should not precede function.

Recognizing the importance of the how as well as the what of the learning experience, instruments should be constructed which would reflect the participant's subjective evaluations of the achievement of learning objectives, the learning experiences (including media) and the learning climate. With the possible exception of climate which is essentially a subjective variable, it is not assumed that participants' subjective assessments measure either the relation between program process (the learning experience) and successful program outcomes, or successful program outcomes in themselves. What does occur, is the collection of information of value in refining further training designs and in modifying or reinforcing the behavior of the training team.

In addition to the questionnaire, exercises can be built into the various program units which provide participants with an opportunity to produce before and after products such as goals and objectives, complete training designs and videotapes of practice sessions. Criteria can be developed to use these products for evaluation purposes. One example of such use is videotapes of practice sessions. Interactional skills cannot be measured by paper and pencil tests, but they can be measured through systematic observation. Those interactional skills of the trainer which are to be stressed can be defined in behaviorally specific terms and placed in categories for coding. Participants can be taught the skills and asked to demonstrate them on videotape. Ratings by the trainer and fellow participants and the videotape itself, in addition to serving as feedback, could also serve as products which could be measures of training outcome.[19]

Realizing that other options are open to evaluators for assessing training outcome, we offer these as suggestions or guides. We are also cognizant of the fact that, while it is essential to measure training outcome, it is even more essential to measure "training transfer to job settings" or "knowledge utilization and dissemination" as this is the ultimate criterion or program effectiveness and training goal achievement. The evaluation of training outcome, as it is used in this model, is a beginning step toward that end.

In summary, the need for trained continuing education specialists in human service is rapidly increasing. Programs created for educating such personnel should be guided by general principles which fall into two categories: <u>what</u> is learned and <u>how</u> it is learned. The training goals, or what is learned, are determined by task analysis which breaks down the terminal task training into a hierarchy of subtasks which are sequenced to permit efficient intratask transfer, enhancing final goal or task accomplishment. The second category of principles concerns the learning process or how it is learned. The key principles governing the learning process and applicable to this model include motivation, practice, modeling, training design and training climate.

These principles are embedded in a model for training beginning trainers which addresses the areas of: selection and assessment of participants; training goals and objectives; training design; trainers; training climate; and evaluation.

The model, as presented in this paper, is intended as a general guide for those concerned with developing or enhancing programs which train trainers.

FOOTNOTES

1. Phyllis Southwick, "Social Work Continuing Education: A Survey of Administrative Structures and Programming in Graduate Schools of Social Work" (unpublished dissertation, the University of Utah Graduate School of Social Work, 1976).

2. Lois Swack, "Continuing Education and Changing Needs," Social Work Vol. 27, No. 6, November 1975, p. 474.

3. Robert Gagne, "Military Training and Principles of Learning," American Psychologist, Vol. 17, 1962, pp. 83-91.

4. Malcolm Knowles, The Modern Practice of Adult Education (New York: Association Press, 1970); and John D. Ingalls, A Trainer's Guide to Androgogy (Washington, D.C.: U. S. Department of Health, Education and Welfare, Social and Rehabilitation Service, 1973).

5. Gagne, 1962, op. cit., pp. 88-96.

6. Robert Gagne, The Conditions of Learning (New York: Holt, Rhinehart and Winston, Inc., 1965), pp. 214-244.

7. John P. Campbell, Marvin D. Dunnette, Edward E. Lawler, and Karl E. Weick, Jr., Managerial Behavior, Performance and Effectiveness (New York: McGraw-Hill, 1970).

8. Gagne, 1962, op. cit.

9. Campbell, et al., op. cit.

10. Gagne, 1965, op. cit.; and Campbell et al., op. cit.

11. Campbell, et al., op. cit., pp. 254-258.

12. Ibid., p. 258.

13. Rolf P. Lynton and Udai Pareek, Training for Development (Homewood, Illinois: Richard D. Irwin, Inc. and the Dorsey Press, 1967), pp. 246-249.

14. Ned A. Flanders, Analyzing Teaching Behavior (Reading, Massachusetts: Addison-Wesley, 1970).

15. Operationalizing the model in ten Basic Training for Trainers courses, we have not found in the literature, interviews with other trainers, or as the result of feedback from participants, any information which would cause us to eliminate or add additional goal areas.

16. Campbell, et al., op. cit.

17. Knowles, op. cit.

18. For a more detailed description of this design, see Matthew Miles, <u>Learning To Work in Groups</u> (New York: Columbia University Press, 1959), p. 234.

19. See Flanders, op. cit.

A Futures Orientation in Program Planning: The Implementation of Peer Teaching among Older Adults in Consumer Education

by Judith L. Warren and Glenn B. McKibbin

Judith L. Warren, M.S., is a doctoral candidate in the Syracuse University School of Education. Glenn B. McKibbin, M.S.W., is Director of the City and County of San Francisco Commission on the Aging; he was formerly Assistant Professor and Associate Director of Community Relations, Field Learning, and Student Affairs of the Syracuse All-University Gerontology Center.

Introduction

Needs assessment, which is most often considered to be a first step in program development, should be, in reality, an ongoing process, integrally related to program design and execution. If needs assessment is used as a first step, one time only, information-gathering tool rather than as an ongoing process, it will be an ineffective base program for design. The reason for this is that valuable information relating to the training of individuals and to the implementation of program goals will be lost. Needs assessment should provide us with a continual flow of information about the various stages of program development. (See Visual 1.)

This paper presents a futures orientation framework for program planning that expands the concept of needs assessment from a first step, one time only, content-oriented inquiry to an ongoing, process-oriented inquiry. This concept focuses on the potential influences whether or not a person uses an idea in the implementation phase that was received in the training phase. Many good program ideas fail in implementation because the needs assessments from which they were developed focused only on content. For

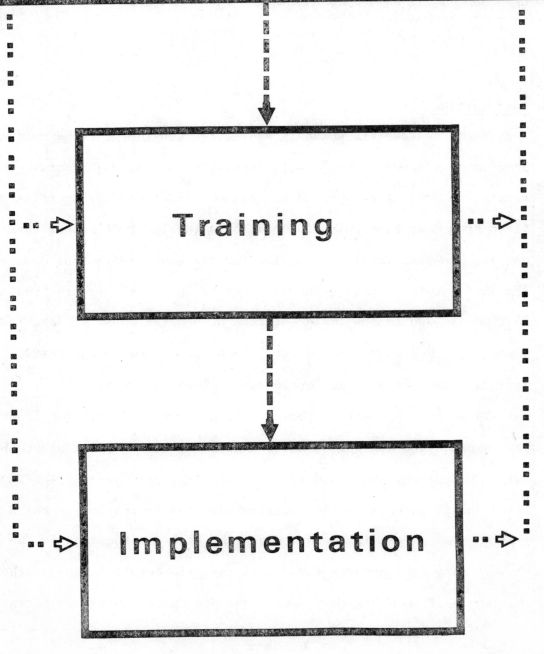

example, in a needs assessment survey, a person may have said "yes, I need to know more about nutrition." A training program developed from this would provide information on the basic four food groups with the intent that the person receiving the training would modify bad food habits to good ones. This goal might not be achieved because there are many things other than knowledge that influence how people act. The needs assessment does not deal with the broader issue of what certain food habits mean to individuals. For instance, a person might not be willing to give up bacon even though she knows that it is high in cholesterol, because having bacon on the table connotes a certain income status.

The futures orientation framework developed out of a search for data to assess needs more accurately in the light of other influences. While the notion of considering the circumstances in which a program takes place is not new to community organization circles, it is to the trainer. It is the notion of systematic inquiry into these circumstances that may be new to both. An examination of the context in which our program development efforts began provides a base for expansion of these ideas.

The Training Context

Seniors Teaching Seniors was a consumer education training program for older adults. A prototype of this training program was developed under federal funding by the New York City Community College and Baruch College-New York State Legislative Institute during the fall of 1976. In the winter of 1977, the training program idea was disseminated to six sites throughout New York state. Syracuse, New York, was one of these preselected sites, and the Syracuse University/All-University Gerontology Center was named as the local sponsoring agency. Let us emphasize that an idea was disseminated. Although broad program goals existed, there were no specific curricula, materials, or training guidelines. Each site was left to custom tailor its own program to meet the major program goals of (1) dissemination of consumer information and (2) training of seniors as consumer educators.

The Seniors Teaching Seniors program is an example of a broader class of programs with the following characteristics:

1. The programs are conceived at the federal or state levels.

2. The sites where the programs are to be held have not been involved in the conception of the idea.

3. The program is funded for a limited period of time with no plan for refunding the specific program.

These characteristics are typical of programs which are meant to bring innovations to a local level. The aims of these programs are often laudable, but the planning approach used to develop them neglects many critical influences on implementation. Implementation here refers not to the training program but to the acceptance and actual use of the training by the trainee once they have returned to their organizational context.

An example may be helpful. In the Seniors Teaching Seniors program one of the goals was to train seniors as consumer education teachers. Think about the implications of this goal. When these individuals were in school, the teacher was the major source of knowledge. There were few outside experts used to enrich the knowledge that the teacher could bring to the classroom. Given this background experience, the senior citizen's notion of teacher might translate into one who is an expert on the topic and is able to give in-depth information on the topic to others. Indeed, when the idea of seniors as consumer education teachers was mentioned to local seniors and to directors of senior centers, the response was one of concern. Some seniors did not feel that they could become teachers, although they were interested in the topic of consumer education. The directors raised the problem of elevating one senior in a center to a teacher role. Other senior center members might not listen to the newly established consumer expert. In this example of one goal's implications, the importance of uncovering such influences as trainee perception and peer acceptance is underscored. Since human service trainees must later function within an organization and within a community, the factors potentially influencing their use of training must be considered in planning.

Individuals and organizations interact within the larger social, political and economic system that we term society. (See Visual 2.) Training programs may be considered as a "force of change"[1] that may affect the entire system for a limited period of time and may modify the relationships within the system. (See Visual 3.) This definition necessarily views training as an innovative process rather than a product in isolation. Training cannot be viewed as it was in our previous example as an "innoculation of nutrition information" that will immunize the trainee from poor eating habits. Training is viewed as an interaction between the trainee, the trainer, the training program and goals, and ultimately the system within which the trainee will function.

The critical factors affecting implementation may then be defined as those variables within the system that interact in the force of change. In the case of seniors becoming teachers, two critical factors were identified: the senior's perception of the role of teacher and peer acceptance of another senior as teacher. Thinking through the implementation process during program planning provides the initial basis for systematically identifying these critical factors. The concept of needs then is recognized as being more complex than a singular need for information or content.

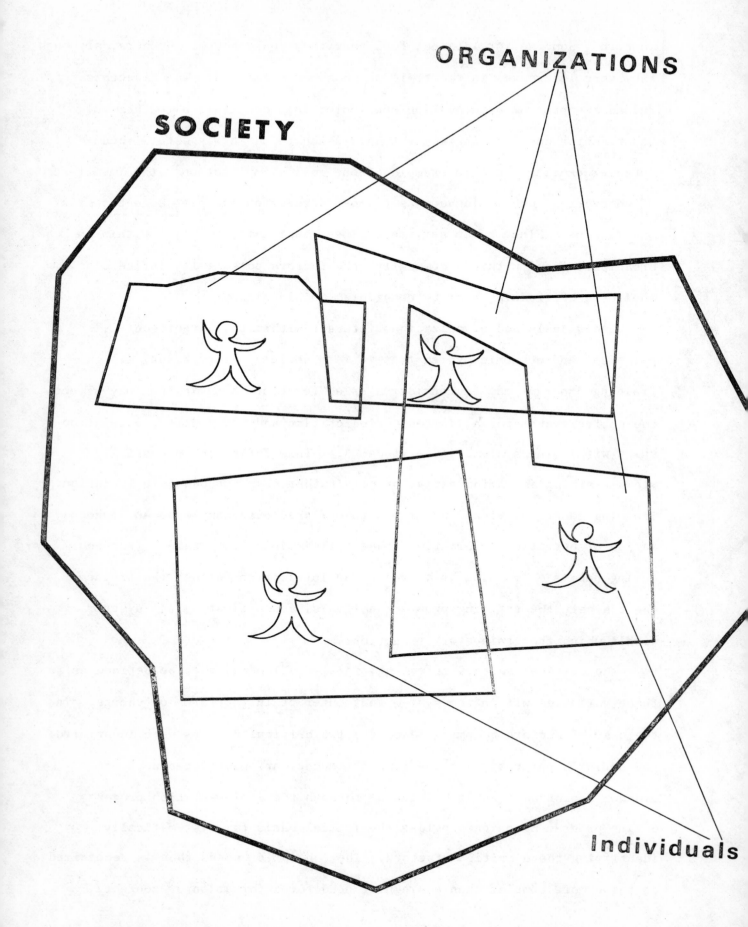

ORGANIZATIONS

SOCIETY

Individuals

ORGANIZATIONS

SOCIETY

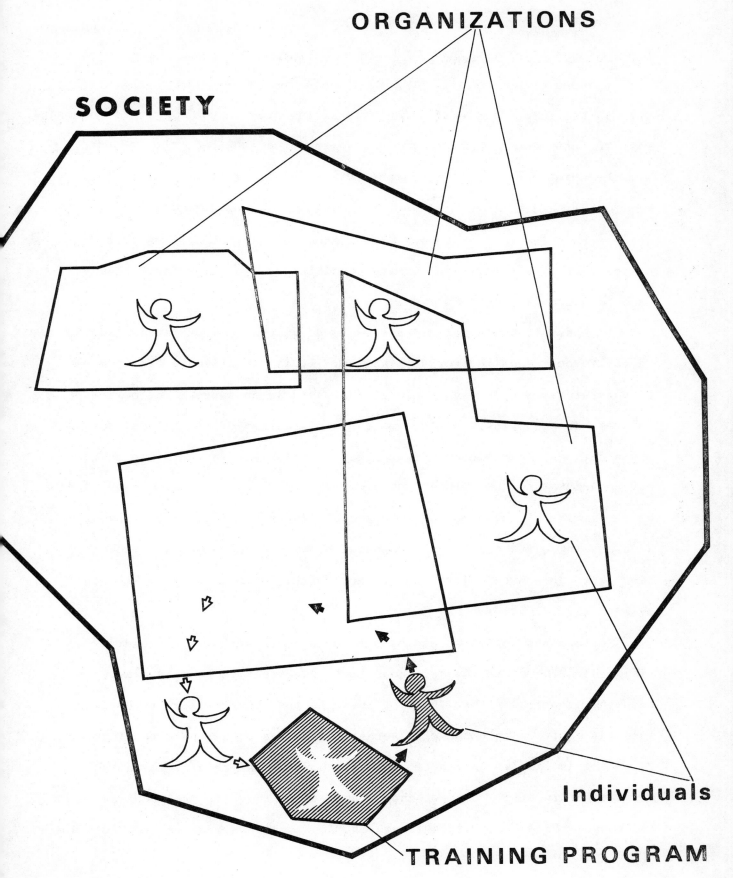

Individuals

TRAINING PROGRAM

Developing a Futures Orientation

Futures orientation in program planning relies heavily on thinking through the future implementation of training program goals. It is concerned with the consequences of program goals--the good, the bad, the intended, and the unintended--that differentiate a futures orientation from other approaches. Although we all know that we cannot look into the future, the attempt to think through future consequences of current actions represents a view that alternative actions are possible and that these actions may lead to quite different futures.

The past looms large in decisions and actions at most levels, whether in public policy or in program planning. It is an influence that those with a futures perspective would like to hold in abeyance. The notion of futures has been viewed by some as the construction of the future; that, given our past, certain occurrences are inevitable. The point is that we have acted toward the future from a coping model. Often we are imprisoned by the limits of the present without exploring possibilities for the future. We are being quite naive by approaching program development with the assumption that, once people learn how to cope within the existing system, things will be all right.

Our own assumption about the future is best expressed by Hendrik Gideonse: "There are several ideas it is important to keep in mind when thinking about the future. One of these is the desirability of getting into the habit of thinking of alternative futures rather than the future. The point is simply that there are many choices available to use at any given point in time. Each of these can lead us to quite different outcomes, and therefore, quite different futures."[2] Gideonse's idea was the forerunner

of an inventive approach toward the future. By inventing desirable alternative futures, choices and the actions following those choices could intervene
to bring about the desirable alternative. We need to view training programs
as interventions into an existing system and thus attend to the future they
may be influencing. This is primarily why we focus on the implementation
process and the consequences of implementing program goals within a societal
context. Focusing on these areas while planning a program not only increases
the probability of program success but promotes the development of an
alternative future that is desirable.

Factors Influencing Implementation

Identifying critical factors which could influence the implementation
of program goals is an important aspect of the futures orientation in
program planning. The literature on change and implementation reviewed by
Michael Fullan and Alan Pomfret[3] suggests four broad categories of such
factors. These are: characteristics of the innovation; strategies; characteristics of the adopting unit; and characteristics of the macro-sociopolitical
unit.

1.   (See Visual 4.) For our purposes here, characteristics of the
innovation include variables such as the complexity and the explicitness of
changes such as knowledge, skill, attitude, and role. In the Seniors
Teaching Seniors program, one variable was the complexity of the role
change, that of becoming a teacher. From our previous example some seniors
and some center directors had expressed concern that the change required
for a person to become a teacher would be too great, especially if they had
never been one. This role change was perceived as too complex to be accepted.
Having this information prior to program development enabled modification

FACTORS AFFECTING IMPLEMENTATION

★ Characteristics of the Innovation

- Complexity
- Explicitness -what, who, when, how

★ Strategies

- Training Program
- Community Involvement

★ Characteristics of the Adopting Unit

- Trainee
- Trainee's Organization

★ Characteristics of the Macro-Socio-Political Unit

- Incentive System
- Political Complexity
- Resources

of the role. Rather than focusing on becoming a teacher, the training would focus on developing skills as a peer resource person in the area of consumer education. This role was perceived as less complex and more congruent with a person's everyday role as information sharer.

2.   (See Visual 4.) Strategies for implementation include the training program, participation via needs assessment, community and organization involvement, resources and follow-up, and feedback. The Seniors Teaching Seniors Training program format was developed using suggestions from both seniors and senior center directors. By incorporating potential trainees' concerns with session length and frequent breaks, the program format was more appropriate. In this example, a participatory strategy that involved only the senior center directors might have resulted in a program format that was less responsive to the seniors' needs.

3.   (See Visual 4.) Characteristics of the adopting unit is further specified as characteristics of the individual trainee and characteristics of the trainee's organization. The characteristics of the trainee would include attitudes, beliefs, skills, and knowledges; cohort or age group; and perception of training. In the example given earlier, the cohort to which the seniors belonged had a different perception of what becoming a teacher would mean.

The characteristics of the trainee's organization would include climate, demographics, and personnel. Determining the climate or environmental support within senior organizations was necessary for developing both training content and implementation strategy.

4.   (See Visual 4.) Characteristics of the macro-sociopolitical unit include the incentive system, the political complexity, and the availability of resources. Analyzing the incentive or reward structure within the local

aging network was critical in predicting what implementation strategies would be most effective.

In the Seniors Teaching Seniors program, the innovation or program goals were largely influenced by the characteristics of the trainees and the dynamics of their organizations. The strategy for training, including the program content and instructional process, was influenced by these factors as well as the incentive system of the "aging" political community. The interdependence of each of these variables on the other is very complex. The interrelationships cannot easily be sorted out into discrete, measurable entities. It is only by attempting to sort out systematically the critical factors influencing implementation that the planning process can be attuned to reality.

Because we are concerned with the planning of a program, we view both the innovation and the strategy as manipulable factors. With the futures orientation, the manipulation would involve conscious decisions and choices on the part of those involved in program planning. It is only through conscious decisions about these factors and the desirable alternative futures that program planning can become a responsive and responsible process.

Utilization of the Futures Orientation Framework

A futures approach to program planning requires that individuals and organizations be willing to surrender part of their autonomy and to deal with the uncertainties involved in order to achieve something of potential value to all. As Donald N. Michael points out: "Although there are very small beginnings within a few organizations of trying to design and implement long range planning there is essentially no planning that looks to alternative futures for the society in which these groups hope to operate and then alters present corporate goals and styles to attain or avoid these futures."[4]

Experience shows that goal setting in future program development is generally too narrow and the interrelationships and their characteristics of organizations are ignored. Plans are founded on simple projections of current values and conditions. In this regard, Michael states, "Generally speaking, the present so preoccupies agency personnel that the future is left to take care of itself."[5]

Characterisitcs of Macro-Sociopolitical Unit

In utilizing the futures orientation framework, the examination of the sociopolitical and economic networks focused primarily on local agencies and organizations providing services for older persons. Those parties or organizations which should be engaged in the process of program planning could then be determined.

This was congruent with a futures orientation in that persons and organizations ultimately affected by a training program were involved in establishing a structure for mutual planning, implementation and evaluation of the training program. The structure in this case was called a steering committee. It was composed of a representative of the Area Agency on Aging, who was responsible for providing professional leadership in the development of senior centers and clubs, several directors of senior centers and clubs, representative of urban and rural environments, the director of an older person's self-advocacy group, a recreational practitioner serving the institutionalized elderly, and several older persons who were members of clubs and centers. The committee reflected the social, political and economic characteristics of the system within which the training program would take place.

The sponsoring agency recognized the political importance of reaching-out to the Area Agency on Aging and inviting its participation as a cosponsor of the Seniors Teaching Seniors program, since it was already working closely with most organizations serving the age group that the training program was designed to reach. The Area Agency on Aging was pleased to be a cosponsor. The program coincided with the agency's goals in providing educational opportunities for older persons, required no additional alloca- tion of financial or manpower resources, and increased the agency's visibility in the community. The primary sponsoring agency benefited by gaining greater credibility in the community through the cosponsorship of the Area Agency on Aging. The Area Agency on Aging professional staff helped to inform the potential audience about the training program through telephone contacts, the Agency's senior center and club mailing list. In addition, the Agency's Council of Senior Centers and Clubs provided the opportunity to interpret the intent of the consumer education training program to the council's older adult members. Council participants could then share this information with their constituent groups of older persons.

Thus, the strategies for program development in part were determined by the characteristics of the macro-sociopolitical system and in part influenced the system by their participatory nature. By recognizing the integration of agencies serving the elderly's interest, training program goals could be developed that were congruent with these interests.

The Steering Committee helped to address the following points:

1. What is important "out there" (community of elders).

2. Internal empires and status.

3. Characteristics of the individual trainee.

4. Development of training goals and instructional means.

Characteristics of the Organization

1. Consideration of What is Important "Out There"

This mutual planning mechanism provided a way to deal with uncertainties in the assessment of consumer education needs of the older adult in the local community. The sponsoring agency believed that the organizations were ready and able to deal with uncertainty because previous political and social relationships had shown the committee members they could trust each other and, as Michael put it, their relevant constituencies allowed them to propose goals and the means for reaching them, which were "original, tentative and subject to revision as the organization environment moved into that future--a future in part invented by their actions and in part imposed by actions of others."[6]

2. Dealing with Empires and Status

The sponsoring agency's philosophical approach to program development was one of planning with and not for participating organizations, thereby supporting and fostering a climate of trust and acceptance. Further, a reciprocal method of intervention was used by the sponsoring agency during the steering committee meetings, wherein the chairperson was influencing committee members and at the same time was influenced by them. In other words, this leadership approach in the planning process showed that power and influence operate much like love--"The more you give away, the more you have." Through the Steering Committee, a synergistic force was at work, in that power and resources were shared for the greater benefit of all.

Other dimensions of the organization were considered:

Participation: The necessity of the system to satisfy individual behavioral needs (security, belonging, esteem, self-actualization) so that large numbers of persons act in concert to obtain the overall goals of the organization was considered. For example, the organization which has an older person participating in the educational program must be a motivating force throughout the older person's educational experience.

Climate: The organization should encourage the older person to share information about the educational program which would be useful to the members of the organization as well as help to satisfy the goals of the organization.

Resources: The circumstances under which the resources of the organization are made available to the member should be specified. For example, before the older person decides to particpate in the educational program, he/she would know to what resources the organization would provide in support of their participation.

3. Characteristics of Trainee

Assessing the characteristics of potential trainees was paramount in the planning activity. The elderly themselves are in a unique position to assess the needs and desires of the older population. The older person's participation promotes self-determination. The elderly had a managing interest in the steering committee and a commitment to the training program and strategy. Participation on the steering committee gave older persons direct involvement in program planning. Their personal needs, values and goals were considered together with their need to be treated with respect. The learning situation was approached in the perspective of the here and now related by the need of their social situation. The older adult played a direct role both in the content (what would be learned) and in the process of choosing (how and when the learning would take place). As Malcolm S. Knowles states, "There is a kind of fundamental law of human nature involved here, which is that any person tends to feel committed to any decision or activity to the extent he has influenced the decision or activity."[7]

Among the more prominent individual level variables included were the valences of the individual for various organizational outcomes and the expectations learned about the circumstances under which he/she would or would not receive various outcomes. For example, one of the aims of the program was to differentiate the functions and roles of the manager of the organization and that of the older person participating in the training program and then to help both learn ways in which they could collaborate to provide information that would improve the quality of life for the members of their organization. Also considered was the level of the individual's skill, the amount of personal energy available to the individual and the degree of psychological stimulation the individual experiences in the organization. For example, the program helped older adults to increase their self-awareness to determine their own limitations and to compensate by drawing on the appropriate resources in the organization and the community at large.

One of the basic aims of the Seniors Teaching Seniors consumer education program was to create a network of interdependence, to help older trainees to function at their fullest capacities to achieve some control over their own personal well-being and environment. Related to this program goal of interdependence was the recognition of the social need to participate and contribute as an individual to the life of the community.

4. Development of Training Goals and Instructional Means

The trainer (lead teacher) functioned as part of the steering committee of a teaching/learning team. The group matured and began to work as a unit as it dealt with the development of the training goals and means of instruction.

As the steering committee formed, it was conceived with its own environment (climate, joint-cooperation, and diverse needs). As the steering committee functioned over time, members started to concern themselves with objectives, such as, "What are we going to do?" and design issues, such as, "How are we going to do it?" and, "With whom?" When the committee reached this new stage in its development, it shifted focus from self-oriented concerns to a position of thinking about others.

Once the committee members felt free to contribute and exchange ideas, with appropriate clarification, the design for training began to take shape. Subsequently, the committee defined with some clarity the general training objectives, and, from these, a set of specific objectives were drawn up that were clearly identifiable and could be measured in behavioral terms when the design was implemented. At this stage, roles and responsibilities were clarified. Certain members of the committee then decided what part they wanted to perform in implementing the design.

Needs and training objectives were planned, in part, through a questionnaire instrument assessing the content needs of the potential participants in the training program. When the training program began, the participants were involved in the process of evaluation—both individually and collectively—fulfilling the need to discuss and share their perception of what was happening.

A number of different instructional formats, devices and skills were used for learning. Formats included individual study, small groups, action projects, etc. Devices included slides, 16 mm. film, tape recordings, flip charts, chalk boards, lectures, buzz groups, simulations, role playing, etc. Trainer skills included the ability both in speaking and writing, audio-visual equipment techniques, group process skills, educational design skills, skills in applied andragogy, etc.

Conclusion

We have attempted to describe a futures orientation to program planning that systematically attends to factors affecting the future implementation of program goals. Our own use of this orientation has included assessment of many of the critical factors identified above. We determined the success of this partial application of futures planning by the results of the implementation phase. That phase is now in process. Success is reflected in the various uses of training by individual trainees in their organizations. For example, two seniors from the Syracuse Consumer Affairs Office started a monthly column entitled "Older and Wiser," which is geared to sharing consumer information gained in Seniors Teaching Seniors. More important, the column is based on questions raised directly by the older consumer in the community. Two seniors for a local senior center have conducted dramatizations of common frauds and cons affecting older people. Another senior made a formal presentation to her organization on prescription drugs. In developing her format she was aware of the needs of her peers. Yet other individuals are utilizing their new consumer information daily: "I spread the information daily in my contact with co-workers. Always a situation reaches my ears where I can volunteer the information I absorbed at our meetings."

These examples represent new behavioral roles on the part of individual trainees. The supportive role of center directors was apparent. In addition, this support has been expressed by the Area Agency on Aging who cosponsored the Seniors Teaching Seniors consumer education program. The Area Agency on Aging has now taken steps to facilitate the ongoing development of consumer education for older adults in the Syracuse area.

The implementation of consumer education reflects the futures orientation process that was the foundation of the program planning.

FOOTNOTES

1. Donald P. Ely, Creating the Conditions for Change (paper presented at the Allerton Park Institute for Graduate School of Library Science, University of Illinois, November 1976).

2. Hendrik, D. Gideonse, "Curriculum Realities," Contemporary Thoughts on Public School Curriculum, E. Short and G. Marconnit, editors (Dubuque, Iowa: William C. Brown Company, 1968), p. 352.

3. Michael Fullan and Alan Pomfret, "Research on Curriculum and Instruction Implementation," Review of Educational Research, Vol. 47, No. 1, 1977, pp. 335-397.

4. Donald N. Michael, On the Social Psychology of Organizational Resistance to Long-Range Social Planning (paper presented at the I.E.E.E. Workshop on National Goals, Science Policy and Technology Assessment, Warrenton, Virginia, April 1972), p. 581.

5. Ibid.

6. Ibid.

7. Malcolm S. Knowles, "Innovations in Teaching Styles and Approaches Based upon Adult Learning," Journal of Education for Social Work, Spring 1972, p. 38.

BIBLIOGRAPHY

Beattie, Walter M., Jr. The Frontiers Of Aging. Paper presented at the National Council on the Aging 24th Annual Meeting, Detroit, Michigan, September 1974.

Ely, Donald P. Creating The Conditions For Change. Paper presented at the Allerton Park Institute Graduate School of Library Science, University of Illinois, November 1976.

Fullan, Michael, and Alan Pomfret. "Research on Curriculum and Instruction Implementation," Review of Educational Research, Vol. 47, No. 1 (1977), pp. 335-397.

Gideonse, Hendrik D. "Curriculum Realities." Contemporary Thoughts on Public School Curriculum, E. Short and G. Marconnit, editors. Dubuque, Iowa: William C. Brown Company, 1968. Pp. 351-356.

Ingalls, John D. A Trainers Guide to Andragogy. Washington, D.C.: United States Department of Health, Education and Welfare, Social and Rehabilitation Service, (SRS) 73-05301, May 1973.

Knowles, Malcolm, S. "Innovations in Teaching Styles and Approaches Based upon Adult Learning," Journal of Education For Social Work (Spring 1972).

Marien, Michael, and Warren L. Ziegler, (eds.). The Potential of Educational Futures. Charles A. Jones Publishing Company: 1972.

Michael, Donald N. On The Social Psychology of Organizational Resistances to Long-Range Social Planning. Paper presented at the I.E.E.E. Workshop on National Goals, Science Policy, and Technology Assessment. Warrenton, Virginia: April 1972.

Porter, Lyman W., Edward E. Lawler, and Richard J. Hackman. Behavior in Organizations. New York: McGraw-Hill Book Company, 1975.

Rogers, Everett M., and F. Floyd Shoemaker. Communication Of Innovation: A Cross-Cultural Approach. New York: The Free Press, 1971.

Schwartz, William. "The Social Worker in the Group," New Perspectives On Services To Groups: Theory, Organization, Practice. New York: National Association of Social Workers, 1961. Pp. 7-29.

Witkin, B. Ruth. An Analysis of Needs Assessment Techniques for Educational Planning at State, Intermediate, and District Level. Hayroard, California: Alameda County Superintendent of Schools, ERIE Document, Reproduction of Services No. ED 108 370.

Zaltman, Gerald, Robert Duncan, and Jonny Holbek. Innovations and Organizations. New York: John Wiley and Sons, 1973.

SIMSWRK (Simulated Social Work): A Systems Simulation of Representative Community and Agency Intervention Experiences

by Max Casper

Max Casper, M.S., M.S.S., is Associate Professor at the Syracuse University School of Social Work.

A major challenge to educators in the human services is finding an appropriate single vehicle for learning that can provide the gestalt of intervention in community, agency, and family life, and that can also respect and enhance the range of individual learning needs of the adults who are in training. One response to this challenge comes from simulation games that are expansive enough in concept to generate some of the key issues of the real world are, at the same time, sensitive enough in format to explicate the educational principles of androgogy. In other words, simulation games should be able to support personal autonomy, provide immediacy of feedback, a sense of accomplishment, and visible relevance to professional life.[1] Furthermore, by their design, simulation games that are used in human services training encourage integration of course work, experience, and philosophy.

At Syracuse University School of Social Work, we tried to meet such a challenge. During the summer of 1971, a team of interested students and faculty met to develop for the incoming first-year graduate students an orientation experience that would raise questions about social workers' activities, enhance the foundation course in Social Work Practice, and prepare the students for entrance into field instruction placements. The outcome of the effort was SIMSWRK--Simulated Social Work.

This paper will review the specific rationale for SIMSWRK, the details of playing the game and running the game from the facilitators' viewpoints, and will give an impressionistic assessment of outcomes and next steps related to some of the current wisdom about simulation games.

The Rationale For SIMSWRK

The rationale for the development of SIMSWRK was threefold: to epitomize the universal concepts and principles of social work practice that emerge as the core of social work education; to use a vehicle for this learning a format that meets the criteria of a well-designed simulation game; and to explicate this simulation experience within the philosophical precepts of androgogy (education of adults).

Historically, the idea of a social work simulation game followed the introduction of SIMSOC (simulated society) to one of the classes at the Syracuse University School of Social Work early in 1971. SIMSOC was sophisticated, exciting, and satisfying to play. However, SIMSOC seemed to touch only peripherally the philosophical base of social work intervention. A simulation, if specifically oriented to social work, could provide a common experience, a common point of reference for illustrating a host of concepts and principles. Concomitantly, such a game would allow the school, students, and faculty alike to get to know each other through a far wider range of dimensions than is usually afforded in beginning school relationships.

The outcome of this motivation was the designing of SIMSWRK, a simulation developed to meet three sets of concrete learning objectives. The first objective for the game was to elicit actions and curiosities among the participants about the universal concepts of the helping process which were being presented in the Social Work Practice I course. These were the building blocks, the basic skills of all practice that were being taught at that time to all first-year students before they made choices of practice concentrations in work with individuals and families, or groups, or community organization and social planning. These universal concepts relate to (1) communication skills, (2) problem solving and conflict management, (3) the formation of helping relationships, and (4) data collection and analysis.

The second objective for SIMSWRK was to engage the players in role taking at the three functional levels: (1) direct service, (2) nondirect service[2] and/or (3) policy and planning.

The last objective was to engage the players in all four service modes: (1) analytic (alone), (2) one-to-one (face-to-face), (3) group (face-to-face), and (4) media-based (out of sight but in communication through messenger, phone, letter, newspaper, etc.)

Having identified the overall problem—the need for a lively all-encompassing experience for the incoming graduate students—and having established some specific objectives—engaging the participants in the application of universal helping concepts at different functional levels and through the four service modes—we were ready to tackle the specifics of the game itself.

In reality, the design of SIMSWRK did not follow such neat and logical order. It is apparent in retrospect, however, that we considered almost all the factors suggested by Francis D. Atkinson, in his systematic approach to designing simulation game activities.[3] The steps noted are: problem statement, objective specification, alternative strategies (games and other activities), identify constraints, selection of strategy, simplified model, identify actors, actors' objectives, actors' resources, events/interaction sequence, winning criteria, establish rules, participants' manual, administrators' manual, implementation, evaluation, and modification.

In our enthusiasm for the prospect of an all-school game, we ignored any consideration of alternative instructional strategies for achieving the same objectives, what alternative could possibly compare with the excitement of the game? We negotiated with the faculty to use an entire day at the end of the first week of orientation, and one entire building at University College (Syracuse University's Continuing Education component). The building was available because of the choice of timing (before classes had started for the semester), and for the requested participation of the entire first-year class. All interested second-year students and faculty were encourage to come. We even stretched our budget to include a bit of money for computer programming and computer time to compile the game scoring later on. We moved ahead to the design of the actual game itself.

Details of Design

A simplified, realistic model of the world of welfare and social work intervention seemed overwhelming until we decided to limit our interactional focus to agencies and families. We were fully aware that a simulation game is a selective representation of social reality involving reductions in complexity and scale; a simulation is isomorphic to reality. Some components are similar and in the same relationship, but the map is not the territory. It was possible, nevertheless, to choose a representative range of agency options and, with a bit of local research, identify the real-world elements that were to be a part of the agency operations in the game.

In this game, participants choose either agency membership or family membership roles. In the first round of play, participants meet in their respective groups as separate units either to create agency structure and policy or to generate family profiles and strategy around identified concerns. In succeeding rounds, agencies provide service. Immediately after each contact (episode of service), participants assess each other's skills on a checklist (Resource Rating Card) concerned with interpersonal relationships. These cards serve as ongoing feedback indicators of perceived effectiveness.

We developed four agencies—the department of social services, department of probation, a community action program, and a settlement house—that could be interactional and provide the range of interventions desired in our objectives. We specified a variety of family structures, including multiproblem families, alternative life styles, foster families and the like. Other actors included the game steering committee and game guides who provided unanticipated events and consequences through a dittoed newsletter published periodically through the game. Also, we developed a change procedure to be used for all family or agency decisions that would hypothetically include interaction with elements of the community beyond the designated players (other agencies, institutions, government units, neighbors, stores, factories). However, by formalizing the deliberate steps in the external decision process (through use of a decision sheet), practice of decision-making skills was incorporated into the game.

To assure that each actor determined his/her personal game goal, the first round of play was designated for planning individual, family, and agency goals and anticipated strategies for interactions between agency and family the "Family Goals Sheet" and the "Agency Organization and Goals Sheet.[4] This format provided clearly established objectives for the actors as well as presenting the opportunity for practice of the fundamental skills.

The last major element in the design of the simulation—the generation of actors' resources—is perhaps the most unique and potentially powerful element in SIMSWRK. This feature is the "Resource Rating Card," which each player carries and uses to assess the actions of every person contacted during the successive playing rounds.[5]

Some of the factors considered to be pertinent to interpersonal competence and relationships are inherent in the six components listed on the card. These are:

1. Time given
2. Information given
3. Esteem shown
4. Energy generated (within you, the assessor)
5. Influence on you (as you perceive it)
5. Expertise used (agency players only)[6]

Assessors rate fellow players 0 (not relevant), 10 (low), 20, 30, 40, 50 (high). "Winning" means getting relatively high scores from your fellow players.

In order to provide early feedback on individual achievement and to demonstrate the power of statistics, a supplementary resource, the computer console was moved in for the day. In between rounds, the computer was used to average scores for each player to help in self-analysis of ratings given by their colleagues.

Action

Actual play of the SIMSWRK game follows the sequence of events and interactions shown on the accompanying flow chart (Figure 1). At the end of preliminary orientation to explain the game and answer questions (in a school or agency setting, this can sometimes be done well in advance of scheduled playing time), players choose a Family or an Agency group. During Round One (one-half hour to an hour), each family meets in its

FIGURE 1

FLOW CHART
SIMSWRK (Simulated Social Work Game)
FALL 1977

PRELIMINARY   ORIENTATION

                          Explanations/Questions
                        Choose Family or Agency Group

Round 1
PLANNING   Family   Agency

                  Choose Roles   Assign Roles
                  Determine Goals   Determine Agency Policies
                  Determine Tactics   and Strategies
                  Send Copy to   Determine Tactics
                                    GAME   Send Copy to
                                    GUIDE
                  External Decisions   External Decisions
                  Assess Family Members with   Assess Agency Members
                    Resource Rating Cards (RRC)   with RRC

Round 2
ENGAGEMENT   Interaction Episodes

                  Family Members go to   Agency Staff go to
                    Agencies   Families
                  Assess Staff Members   Assess Family Members
                    after Each Contact   after Each Contact
                    Episode   Episode

                                    GAME
                  External Decisions GUIDE   External Decisions

                  END OF ROUND   END OF ROUND

            ⬆ No   Yes   Yes   No ⬆
                             ⬇   ⬇

TOWN MEETING   Debriefing: Each Group Report Highlights
                               Clarify Questions of Play

Round 3   (Add Imaginary Time Passage)
                  -Plan   -Plan
                             -Interact

EVALUATION   Subjective Impressions/Formal Feedback Checklist
                  Turn in RRCs, Goals and Decision Sheets

-121-

"home" and chooses individual roles.[7] They then proceed in character to determine personal game goals, decide on tactics for contact with one of the four agencies in the game during the succeeding rounds. They make an external decision by stating on the Decision Sheet the question or action that is a problem and that cannot be decided within the family or game agencies, and three or more alternative action decisions. The family members take this filled-out decision sheet to the nearest Game Guide, who will, by change, determine which decision option is to pertain. Players then proceed as if the option had happened. At the end of the round, family members fill out their Resource Rating Cards and rate every person with whom they have interacted, using the identification code numbers assigned to each player. The families turn in the cards to the Game Guide, who will submit them to the computer operator for processing. Copies of the family and agency goals sheets are also given to the Game Guide, so the Game Steering Committee can know what is being established.

Meanwhile, down at their "offices," agency members are assigning roles at various levels (director, supervisor, worker), determining policies and strategies, using the external decision process with the Decision Sheets and the Game Guides wherever appropriate, and deciding on tactics for meeting family needs in the upcoming round. These "staff" people also assess each other at the end of the first round.

Round Two begins with players interacting, rating each other, and using game guides for external decisions. Between Rounds Two and Three, a "Town Meeting" is held whereby each group can report the highlights of the interactions and clarify with the Game Steering Committee any questions about how to play.

Round Three begins with the announcement of an imaginary passage of time (a day, week, month later). Action begins back in home or office groups with planning and subsequent engagement similar to the previous round.

SIMSWRK is climaxed by the Evaluation Session, where impressionistic and formal protocols reinforce learning from the simulation experience.

Supporting Factors

To support the game action, various rules of play and criteria for winning were established and incorporated into manuals for the participants (agency and family players) and for the administrators (Steering Committee and Game Guides). Basically, the criteria for winning were kept very informal and intrinsic to the action and relied primarily on the players' discovery of personal motivation to improve scores on the Resource Rating Cards from round to round or from interaction to interaction. Therefore, manufacturing a total Group Score from individual rating scores was deemed superfluous. Realistically, the prevailing educational values emphasized playing rather than winning for its own sake.

Procedural rules that placed limits on play were only two. The first rule encouraged or exhorted the participants to stay in role throughout the round. Family members were asked first to develop and then to maintain their character portrayals at all times. Similarly agency people were expected to be a particular staff member throughout. The second rule implemented the use of the Decision Sheet for external devisions in those circumstances that depended on a role outside the realm of the game roles (for example, other agencies and institutions, members of the extended family, whose actions might impact on players in the game). In accordance with this rule, either family and/or agency players were to fill out the

Decision Sheet (noting the question to be decided and at least three alternative solutions) and then to bring the plan to one of the Game Guides who
would use a chance method for choosing one soluation.[8] After the choice
was initiated by player and Game Guide, the play proceeded as if the signed
act had happened.[9]

The Participant's Manual contained instructions to players, profiles
of families and the four agencies, and sample copies and explanations of
the forms used in the game. Family member roles were derived in some
detail from the actual circumstances of families known to the committee of
student social workers who initially created the descriptions. Family role
players were asked to present themselves in their characterization through
the choice of a predominant style ranging from functional to dysfunctional
along one of the following four continua: (1) rational to superrational;
(2) blaming to critical; (3) imaginative to purely fantastic; (4) mediating
to merely pacifying.

Agency profiles included background, purpose, programs, and table of
organization so that during the first round of play players could develop a
workable strategy for providing service. The four agencies were department of social services (welfare, human services), probation, settlement
house/neighborhood family service, and community action.

Administrative units, materials and activities were generated to
assure that the game proceeded smoothly, that there were mechanisms to
handle unanticipated consequences, and that the aura of dramatic speciality
was enhanced. The key administrative unit was the Game Steering Committee,
which made spot decisions about timing, who went where, what to do until
the computer came, when and some of what to publish in the Newsletter and
the like. The committee was helped by Game Guides who handled the external

decisions described earlier according to instructions on their instruction sheets; answered players' frantic questions, ran the tape recorders, collected rating cards, and performed other tasks. A key asset was the team that published an on-the-spot Newsletter which helped clarify general instructions and announced unanticipated events planned by the steering committee, such as community forums, strikes, advancing of the calendar and clock, computer results, etc. Agencies and citizens in the game also used the Newsletter to announce the job openings, special meetings for social action, and editorials about the community. This activity added its own unanticipated influences.

Prior to the SIMSWRK "happening," administrative planning meetings were helpful. These meetings coordinated announcement and recruitment for the event, set up rehearsal orientation meetings for the Game Guides, and arranged for the embellishments which added clarity and glamor to the experience. In addition to a program schedule and a chart showing room layout and specifying which group was to meet where, large color-coded title cards were made for identifying agency rooms and family rooms. Name tags were color-coded for different families and different agencies. As a final touch of glamor, a porta-pack video set was available for roving documentation of the "busy agency waiting room," the "street" (corridor) demonstration (families protesting insufficient service), and "family crisis." Agency/family activities were tape-recorded interactions for possible feedback on skills at some future time.

Implementation and Evaluation

In SIMSWRK as in any game, the unknowns and the wide range of variables often lead to unpredictable and unexpected outcomes. For example, SIMSWRK was first played in 1971. It seems that the presence of the porta-pack video equipment in the game, during that particular time in history (just after the activism of the late sixties, including the 1968 Democratic convention in Chicago and a series of citizen demonstrations through community action in Syracuse itself), contributed to a spontaneous role-playing demonstration outside of the Department of Social Services space by the Community Action Program game members--right in front of the video camera.

On the other hand, the planned use of the computer to do the calculations from the Resource Rating Cards and give immediate printouts of individual scores broke down because the time for entering the data took far longer than we anticipated. What was even more surprising was the furor this delay created from enthusiastic players who wanted to know how they were doing (since during the playing round the cards were held by the assessor, not the assessee--a circumstance we changed in subsequent game sessions).

Both these events show that participants were caught up in the "flow" of the experience--an experience that seemed to balance the mix of challenge and ability. As suggested by Mihaly Csikszentmihalyi,[10] high challenge coupled with low ability leads to anxiety; high ability and low challenge can lead to boredom (see Figure 2).

The SIMSWRK evaluation forms used during the premier of the game in 1971 asked students to assess, in consonance with the principles of androgogy, the degrees of education and personal value related to the following: the "building blocks" concepts of social work practice (communication, data collection and analysis, decision-making, facilitative relationships); observation of, or role participation in, direct, indirect, and policy levels of agency service; awareness of role realism; new parameters of agency operation; worthwhileness of the time spent; readiness to recommend further use of the SIMSWRK game.

FIGURE 2

Participation "Flow" As A Locus of
Balance Between Challenge and Ability
(Adapted from Mihaly Csikszentmihalyi, 1975.)

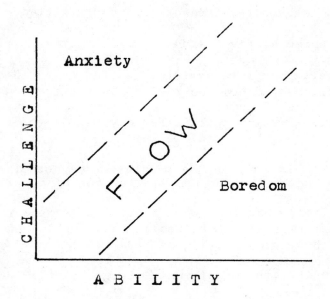

Response from the student participants was generally quite favorable.[11]
Comments supported "the worthwhileness of exposing students to the realities
of the communication process between agencies and clients," and were addressed
to "the sharpening of awareness of the difficulties of communication in
supposedly helping encounters." Students mentioned "beginning to feel the
frustration that people [they would] be working with experience in their
everyday life" and saw the experience as "a good inductive learning exposure
--a way to get at a feeling level in problem solving."

In recent unstructured feedback, students stated similar subjective
impressions on three by five cards:

> "I really got into my role, had fun (as a 15-year old runaway)
> and discovered how you really can get the runaround at times."

> "Everyone really acted like they were into it--you felt like
> you were a real social worker."

> "The simulation went better than I expected; not as complicated
> as one might imagine despite the ton of paper we were given."

> "The family problems were a bit too extreme (although they were
> taken from real sitatuions); less complicated problem situations
> would have made getting started easier."

In the Fall 1977 run of SIMSWRK, the group of 30 undergraduate students
was asked to use a "values clarification" technique for on-the-spot feedback.
Students gave to "living answers" the same questions asked invidually in
former years by lining up behind one of five chairs representing a range
from low to high. Exceptionally high ratings were given to the question of
the extent to which experiences in the game aroused students' questions
about concepts and principles of communication and decision making. Responses
were evenly distributed over the questions about data collection and analysis.
Players reported they were highly active in direct service roles, less so
in administration and policy efforts. The game's realism was also rated
very highly, as was cooperation in interactions on one-to-one, group, and

intergroup levels. Players felt quite confident about their skills as facilitators, less so about their skills in communication and decision making.

Positive recommendation to future incoming students was unanimous. This feedback paralleled previous feedback about SIMSWRK and provided a sound basis for classroom emphasis in the practice courses. Shared experiences thus became a vehicle for integration, confirmation, and criticism of what had been learned and what was ahead.

The use of SIMSWRK for staff training might well produce similar outcomes and responses, although, to date, this has not yet been applied.

Modifications of SIMSWRK

In keeping with the last factor in the Atkinson[12] approach to designing simulation games, experience and circumstance did indeed demand modifications in subsequent playing of SIMSWRK. In 1971, the game was set for the entire entering first-year graduate class during orientation, using a not-yet-scheduled field instruction weekdays, an entire building for a day, and an on-line computer console. Six families and four agencies were created. In 1977 the game was set for two undergraduate classes in Social Services plus interested graduate students. It was run on a Saturday morning with only eight players and on a Tuesday evening with 30, using one large room and several supplementary "small spaces" nearby.

How could SIMSWRK be adapted and still remain intrinsically the same, if not better, educationally? The Game Steering Committee (two faculty with the added input from three graduate students) decided on one family instead of several, and one agency (the three graduate players) with flexible "outreach" potential. Therefore, whenever a "client" approached an unattended "agency" table, one of the three graduate students went over to that table to answer the call, assumed the relevant role for that agency, and proceeded to offer service to the "client" making active use of the Decision Sheets and Game Guides (faculty) to answer hypothetical external questions.

The major innovation, induced by the need to overcome the cumbersome use of the computer in the original version, was to reverse the ownership of the Resource Rating Card. Each assessee retained possession of her/his own card, and marked her/his code identification on top of the card. At the end of each episode, players exchanged cards, rated each other, then retrieved their cards before movin on to the next action. The advantages of this system were that each player received immediate feedback on perceptions by the other player(s), and each player could easily sum personal scores, thus eliminating the need for a computer (except for programming for research purposes at some future time). Another change was that with small groups, we resorted to the use of the chalkboard as a substitute for a dittoed newsletter to announce time lapses, modified procedures and other events.

One recommendation for further improvement in SIMSWRK gaming with future classes include (1) staging a "dry run" in the classroom prior to the actual game play, if possible. This would reduce the amount of new information to be absorbed on the day of play. Also, explaining the appropriate use of and significance of the Resource Rating Card, including a step-by-step demonstration, was recommended to alleviate confusion. Furthermore, it was suggested that the manual of instruction for players and administrators be made more concise but include an index and appendix for further elaboration.

Summary and Current Wisdoms About Simulation Games

SIMSWRK models the total system of social work delivery. The selected, representative parts of community and agency connect to and affect each other within arbitrary but realistic boundaries. As Robert Ohm noted, "most total system simulations [including SIMSWRK] are of the open system type in which some of its structure and process emerge or develop during the course of play."[13] These dynamics are much more functional and more like the real world than a "closed system" model, which would attempt to control every known move.

With the open system simulation, however, comes a mixture of gains and limitations. Some of the stated values of simulation include: production of high motivation and efficacy, development of skills, rehearsal of responsibilities, increased sympathy/empathy for people and their circumstances, deeper understanding of group processes, reality testing, conceptual learning, learned flexibility. Limiting risks, on the other hand, include oversimplification, too much motivation for some, reinforcement of the "wrong" values, dehumanization, dysfunctional attitudes, inappropriate prerequisites based on alien roles and skills undue classroom control.[14] Thus far, SIMSWRK seems to have generated more assets than limitations.

Simulation tends to produce more student motivation and interest, but studies show no significant differences in learning retention, critical thinking, or attitudinal changes.[15] Therefore, we are obliged, at present, to build our enthusiasms for simulation gaming on "feel" and intuition, not on hard research. This mixed perspective is confirmed by a rather extensive exploration of current simulation gaming research by Hunter and Clark. But their report is presented with the caveat that in such research "it is extremely difficult to control such factors as length of play, size of

playing group, assignment given in addition to the game, individual players'
abilities, administrative abilities of the directors, effects caused by
role assignments, and activities of the control groups."[16] In other words,
since there are still heavy methodological limitations on the research
procedures per se, our other bases for support of simulation are admissible.

Our strongest support for SIMSWRK came from the participants who
enjoyed role-playing as family or agency members. They gained fresh insights
from both giving and receiving immediate and ongoing feedback provided by
the use of the Resource Rating Cards, since these cards focused on their
interpersonal social work skills. They appreciated being treated educationally as adults. The educators/designers assumed that the students were
healthy, mature equals, who were expected to interact as persons, not as
objects. The educational milieu created a here-and-now, process-oriented
model of freedom within limits. Mutual efforts between educator and participants encourage creativity, experimentation and permissiveness for the
latter.[17]

SIMSWRK easily accomodates a varied number of participants. It is
also responsive to differing needs assessments and timing. When used in
the beginning of a training period--for orientation of incoming students or
staff, for example--it serves as a common experiential referent upon which
to build. Used later in a shared experience, the simulation serves as a
vehicle for integration, criticism or confirmation of what has been learned.
Regardless of the particular learning objective, the simulation activity
demonstrates the underlying gestalt of social work and other human services.

FOOTNOTES

1. Malcolm Knowles, "Innovations in Teaching Styles and Approaches Based upon Adult Learning," Journal of Education for Social Work, Vol. 8 (Spring 1972), p. 2.

2. Nondirect service is meant as a "neutral term" which includes professional responsibility by a helping person who is at least once removed from the beneficiary of service (the client unit), but who is responsible for the behaviors of a direct service worker (through supervision, consultation, staff development, team leadership, etc.).

3. Francis D. Atkinson, "Designing Simulation/Gaming: A Systems Approach," Journal of Educational Technology, Vol. 17 (February 1977), pp. 38-43.

4. Data requested on planning sheets for families and agencies:

FAMILY GOALS SHEET

Member Code #	Last Name	First Name	Family Role	Personal Goal	Strategy Plan for next Round

Family Goal:

Family Strategy for next round:

(Please file one of 2 copies with your Family Game Guide)

AGENCY ORGANIZATION AND GOALS SHEET

Agency:
Agency Game Goals:
Table of Organization:

Member Code #	Last Name	First Name	Role

(Please file one of 2 copies with your Agency Game Guide)

5. <u>SIMSWRK Resource Rating Card</u> Information:

Please rate each player 0 (not relevant) or 10 (low), 20, 30, 40, 50
(high) on each item after each contact episode:

Assessor Code #
Assessee Code #
Clock time (into the round)
Location (Group #)

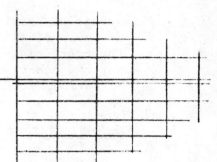

1. Time Given
2. Information Given
3. Esteem Shown
4. Energy Generated (within you)
5. Influence on You
6. Expertise Used (rate <u>AGENCY</u> players only)

6. <u>Resource Rating Cards: Definitions and Standards</u>

a. <u>Time Given</u> (for interaction). Consider:
   <u>Real time</u> spent in interaction by the other player (the Assessee)
   too short, too long, just right.
   <u>Undivided attention</u> – the degree to which the Assessee paid you
   (the Assessor) undivided attention, allowed interruptions, or
   was distracted for periods of time.

b. <u>Information Given</u> (how were your questions answered?). Consider
   to what extent:
   your questions were answered distinctly;
   the informant volunteered information;
   the informant gave you superfluous or irrelevant information.

c. <u>Esteem Shown</u> (toward you). Consider the player's (Assessee's):
   regard for your desires; apparent respect for your ideas;
   apparent belief in your ability to succeed;
   ability to inspire your self-confidence.

d. <u>Energy Generated</u> (within you) by the Assessee. Consider the extent
   to which:
   the Assessee gave you hope and motivation.
   you (the Assessor) became enthused, inspired, stimulated by the
   Assessee to further action of your own.

e. <u>Influence</u> over you. Consider the extent to which:
   the Assessee induced you to a commitment to reach her/his goals;
   you might derive benefit from her/his persuasion/coercion.

f. <u>Expertise Used</u> (rate Agency Members Only). Consider:
   the degree of competence you believe the agency member displayed
   in helping you to cope with your situation;
   your belief that the Assessee's ideas (if any) will work in your
   behalf and are rational.

7. Examples of family role descriptions:

You are a 42-year old mother. Your husband is dying of a terminal illness. You must work to support your family. There is a growing gap between you and your children and you are worried about it. You do not know what is causing the gap.

You are a 50-year old father, dying of a terminal disease. You are still able to live at home but require much nursing care and cannot work. Your wife has taken a job but medical bills cannot be met. She is withdrawing from you. You become more easily frustrated with your children than previously.

You are a 12-year old son. You are having serious difficulties in school. Your grades are failing, you have no friends, you have been truant from school and are in danger of being placed on probation.

8. One method for chance choices asks the player to choose a number 1-100 and a letter A-F, then use the following <u>Decision Choices Chart</u> to pick the number of the Decision Alternative to be followed in the game.

	A	B	C	D	E	F
1-33	1	1	2	2	3	3
34-66	2	3	3	1	1	2
67-100	3	2	1	3	2	1

9. Examples of decision choices:

Situation: A Community Services staff player had referred a youth to a federal job training program.

Question to be decided: How did the youth do on the job?

Hypothetical answers: 1. Specific program was terminated after three weeks.
2. He was doing marginally well, making minimum wage.
3. His father made him quit.

Choices: The staff player cited 69-B, which the Game Guide drew from the Decision Choice Chart to be alternative #2.

Follow up: The staff player and the youth player proceeded on that basis.

10. Mihaly Csikszentmihalyi, <u>Beyond Boredom and Anxiety: The Experience of Play in Work and Games</u> (San Francisco: Jossey-Bass, 1975).

11. Communication, problem-solving skills were rated high; data analysis was low; direct service, realism, new parameters were high; policy awareness was relatively low.

12. F. D. Atkinson, "Designing Simulation Gaming: A Systems Approach," Journal of Educational Technology, Vol. 17, February 1977, pp. 38-43.

13. Robert E. Ohm, "Gamed Instructional Simulation: An Exploratory Model," Educational Administration Quarterly, Vol. 2 (Spring 1966), p. 119.

14. William W. Joyce, "Selecting, Evaluating, and Designing Simulation Games," High School Journal, Vol. 57 (April 1974), pp. 292-311.

15. Cleo Cherryholmes, "Some Current Research on Effectiveness of Educational Simulations: Implications and Alternative Strategies," American Behavioral Scientist (October 1966), p. 7, cited by E. M. Gilliom, High School Journal, Vol. 57 (April 1974), pp. 265-272.

16. Robert Hunter and Richard E. Clark, "Simulation/Gaming Research," Educational Technology, Vol. 17 (July 1977), p. 45.

17. Max Casper, "The Use of the Class as a Group To Teach Group Process," Teaching and Learning in Social Work Education, comp. Marguerite Pohek (New York: Council on Social Work Education, 1970), pp. 43-58.

BIBLIOGRAPHY

Atkinson, F. D. "Designing Simulation/Gaming: A Systems Approach." Journal of Educational Technology. 17:38-43, February 1977.

Bardill, D. R. "Simulated Family as an Aid to Learning Group Treatment." Child Welfare, Vol. 55 (December 1976), pp. 703-709.

Casper, Max. "The Use of the Class as a Group To Teach Group Process" Teaching and Learning in Social Work Education. Compiled by Marguerite Pohek. New York: Council on Social Work Education, pp. 43-58.

Cherryholmes, Cleo. "Some Current Research on Effectiveness of Educational Simulations: Implications and Alternative Strategies." American Behavioral Scientist (October 1966), pp. 4-7, cited by E. M. Gilliom, High School Journal, Vol. 57 (April 1974), pp. 265-72.

Csikszentmihalyi, Mihaly. Beyond Boredom and Anxiety: The Experience of Play in Work and Games. San Francisco: Jossey-Bass, 1975.

Engin, A. W. and Miller, J. N. "Training of School Psychologists through Simulation." Psychology in the Schools, Vol. 12 (January 1975), pp. 40-42.

Ganeles, Dan. "Competency-Based Preparation Programs for Teachers of Adults." Adult Leadership, Vol. 23 (December 1974), pp. 187-189.

Gilliom, E. M. "Trends in Simulation." High School Journal, Vol. 57 (April 1974), pp. 265-72.

Herman, W. L., Jr. "Performance Competencies: Lessons Using a Prototype, Simulation, and Protocol Materials." Part II. Social Education, Vol. 42 (March 1977), pp. 23-26.

Hunter, Robert, and Richard E. Clark. "Simulation/Gaming Research." Educational Technology, Vol. 17 (July 1977), p. 44.

Joyce, William W. "Selecting, Evaluating, and Designing Simulation Games." High School Journal, Vol. 57 (April 1974), pp. 292-311.

Knowles, Malcolm. The Modern Practice of Adult Education: Androgogy vs. Pedagogy. New York: Association Press, 1972.

Knowles, Malcolm S. "Innovations in Teaching Styles and Approaches Based Upon Adult Learning." Journal of Education for Social Work, Vol. 8 (Spring 1972), p. 2.

Knox, A. B. "Higher Education and Life-Long Learning." Journal of Research and Developmental Education, Vol. 7 (Summer 1974), pp. 13-23.

McTernan, E. J. "Androgogical Education in the Health Services." Adult Leadership, Vol. 23 (November 1974), p. 136.

Ohm, Robert E. "Gamed Instructional Simulation: An Exploratory Model." Educational Administration Quarterly, Vol. 2 (Spring 1966) pp. 110-22.

Park, Danbey. "The Cooperative Assessment of Experiential Learning (CAEL)." Adult Leadership, Vol. 23 (February 1975), pp. 242-47.

Steinakes, Norman and Robert M. Bell. "How Teachers Can Use Experiential Taxonomy." Educational Technology, Vol. 16, No. 16 (1976), pp. 49-50.

Stone, G. L. "Effect of Simulation on Counsellor Training." Counseling Education and Supervision, Vol. 14 (March 1975), pp. 199-203.

Taylor, Andrew J. R. "Developing Your Own Simulation for Teaching Social Studies." The Clearing House, Vol. 50 (November 1976), p. 104.

SIMSI: A Simulation
of Services Integration

by Vincent Faherty

Vincent Faherty, D.S.W., is Director of Undergraduate Studies of the University of Missouri-Columbia School of Social and Community Services.

This paper discusses simulation--that unreal phenomenon that attempts to capture, however fleetingly, a moment, a process, an event that has quite real and quite critical consequences for the human service professional. The subject of the simulation is the integration of human services in a community--that elusive goal every profesional seeks as did the sixteenth and seventeenth century explorers search for the mythical fountain of youth in Florida or the navigable water route through America to the Orient. In many ways, true integration of human services is very much like the fountain of youth or the route to the Orient: everyone wants it but very few are willing to hack through the jungle growth to find it.

There is merit to proceed beyond the subject of the integration of human services to the method, the use of simulation and gaming. I propose to briefly discuss the viability of the method of simulation, then present in detail SIMSI (A Simulation of Services Integration), and, finally, project into the future and discuss other uses of the gaming/simulation technique for the training of professionals who serve the community through social work, psychology, education, therapeutic recreation, community development and nursing.

A simulation is "...an operating model of the central features or elements of a real or proposed system, process or environment."[1] It freezes a time, a place or an action and allows the viewer or participant the luxury of entering into that picture, as it were, and sensing its complexities and interrelationships. It is analogous to stopping the life process, as one would stop a video tape play back, and walking around between and among the players to attempt to understand what they are doing and why.

Simulation and gaming have traditionally been used by social scientists, educators and the business community for both education and research. The educational game design

> ...consists generally of a system analysis of the substantive problem, process, or situation to be taught; the design of a logical or mathematical model that is a simplified manipulable analog of the process or problem to be taught; the design of a human player simulation of the model; and the refinement of both the original system analysis and abstract model through repeated test plays of the game.[2]

The employment of simulation for research is even more intriguing. "The scientist studies the model rather than the real life and thereby hopes to learn something about that real life process."[3] Viewed from this research perspective, the use of simulation for human service research opens up vistas that would be unrealistic or unethical when one considers the life situation of a client or population at risk. Unhindered by the risk involved in empirical, scientific research with human subjects, or clients in our terminology, simulation offers an almost limitless range of research and evaluation opportunities within the security of the unreal yet relevant.

In short, simulation occupies the midpoint on the continuum of classroom and the clinical or community practicum experience. Simulations are not hampered by the classroom environment which utilizes the lecture, the Socratic question and answer approach, or the plodding case study attempt at learning. Neither do simulations encroach upon the field instruction or clinical model of instruction, wherein the student is expected to have attained the requisite knowledge, values and skills to be able to interview, intervene and evaluate actual clients, groups or communities.

Such an experience was and is SIMSI--neither classroom nor existential reality. And this phenomenon--neither fact nor illusion--is, I believe, both its limitation and its strength, its constraint and its promise.

Scope

SIMSI is situated in the present time in the community Fagansport, a city of 100,000 people. Within this city the following human service agencies function in response to identified community needs.

AGENCIES

Association for Retarded Citizens

City-County Health Department

City Housing Authority

Division of Family Services

Income Maintenance Unit

Service Unit

Employment Security Office

Family and Children's Services

Individual Counseling Unit

Services Division

General Hospital

    Outpatient Department

    Social Services Department

Homemaker's Services, Inc.

Human Development Association Action Center

Legal Services, Inc.

Mental Health Center

    Individual Counseling Unit

    Services Division

Parks and Recreation Department

Planned Parenthood

Public School System

    Community Education Department

    Social Services Department

Social Security Administration

Fagansport can be considered an average American city in the sense that it is experiencing a typical set of problems relative to economic growth, population expansion, housing and transportation resources, environmental pollution, and community services. There is no one community problem that is emergent. In other words, it is not a city in crisis but is rather one that is developing with a standard amount of resources and constraints to growth.

SIMSI was developed during the summer of 1977 as part of an HEW funded grant entitled, "Human Services Capacity Building," at the University of Missouri-Columbia. The College of Public and Community Services was the recipient of the grant and the School of Social Work, of which I am a faculty member, is administratively part of that College. The grant was focused on the development of capacities, both institutional and individual, for the human service professional to integrate skills, knowledge and values in the delivery of human services. SIMSI was one methodological approach to the overall objective of the grant.

At this point, I propose to discuss SIMSI according to the following framework: objectives, design, preliminary findings, and projections for the future.[4]

Objectives

Within the confines of simulation, as methodology, and integration of humans, as content, the following objectives were developed for SIMSI:

1. To identify the problems relative to communication, efficiency, and effectiveness that exist in and among presently functioning human service agencies.

2. To increase the participants' understanding of the concept "human services integration."

3. To involve the participants in a structured experience which simulates two disparate approaches to human services integration.

4. To provide the environment in which the participants can first evaluate the efficiency and effectiveness of these two approaches to integration of services and then to project alternate models of integrated service delivery.

5. To sensitize the participants to the intricate and complex factors of personality and structure that are present in any attempt to integrate human service systems.

Design

Two distinct approaches to human services integration are simulated in SIMSI. These two approaches are represented as Phase I and Phase II of the exercise.

Phase I simulates the manner in which human services are delivered, in most, if not all, of American communities today. The assumptions underlying Phase I are:

1. Agencies are independent of each other, follow distinct policy guidelines for service delivery, and initiate services through individual agency intake systems.

2. There exists a philosophical commitment to integrate services based on the continuum of client needs.

3. Service integration is attempted through formal channels of referrals by means of intake and informal channels of communication among professional staff.

4. Services integration is aided by means of a community services manual—called the Fagansport Service Coordination Handbook—which lists agencies by function and service resources.

5. Treatment plans are developed by individual human service professionals.

Phase II of SIMSI introduces into the community of Fagansport three radical phenomena:

1. The existence of a Human Service Center—a federally financed central referral agency which possesses the legislative authority, fiscal resources, and community sanction to function as the only intake, assessment and referral agency in the community;

2. The presence of a computer which provides instant access to data regarding what services are available at a particular point in time in the community;

3. The utilization of an assessment team, not individuals, to interview, determine needs, and complete the case treatment plans.

Sequence of Operations

During Phase I participants are divided into two categories of players: Initiating Agents and Service Providers. (See Figure 1.) Five players act as Initiating Agents and perform the function, essentially, of treatment planning. Each Initiating Agent receives a written description of a proto-typical multiproblem family and are asked to: (1) isolate the problems confronting that family; (2) identify what services are needed; (3) identify the appropriate agency for each service required; (4) contact that agency for a referral appointment; and (5) record on the treatment plan the time and date of the appointments.

Fifteen players represent the Service Providers, in other words, those agencies that exist in the simulated community of Fagansport. The Service Providers are the persons contacted by the Initiating Agents for the referral appointments. At the beginning of Phase I, each Service Provider received a detailed description of his/her agency in terms of policies, services, and regulation.

One of the primary rules of simulation and game design is to provide distinct objectives and activities for each player. Thus, during Phase I of SIMSI, in order for the Service Providers not to be simply sitting patiently waiting to be contacted by the Initiating Agents, they too have an objective. The Service Providers' objective is to complete an appointment book for a one-week period. They do this in two ways: first, by

FIGURE 1

PHYSICAL ARRANGEMENT OF PLAYERS DURING PHASE I

Service Providers

Initiating Agents

turning over a series of information cards periodically during the session--information cards which allow the Service Providers to "fill up" their appointment book with staff meetings, telephone referrals, etc. The second way in which Service Providers complete their appointment book is by being contacted by the Initiating Agents for their clients.

Thus, there exists a slight level of tension and somewhat conflicting objectives between the Initiating Agents and the Service Providers. The Initiating Agents need service for their clients and the Service Providers need to complete their appointment books as quickly as possible. It is our hypothesis in developing SIMSI that this tension does exist in reality. In other words, a philosophical commitment to services integration often conflicts with a specific agency's own internal needs, specifically the need to maintain territoriality of professional roles and program responses. The pervasive fear seems to be that it is economic suicide to coordinate and integrate human services, for some programs will end or be restricted while others will expand. SIMSI tries, in a simulated manner, to capture that tension and that disincentive to integrate.

Two criteria for evaluation are utilized during Phase I. Efficiency is gauged by the time it takes the Initiating Agents to complete a treatment plan for each case. (See Figure 2.) Completing a treatment plan involves the entire process from assessment to arrangement of an actual appointment for each service required. The time is measured with a stop watch and recorded.

Effectiveness, the second criteria, is determined by the identification of the number of correct services needed and agencies considered appropriate for the observable problems. What is a "correct" service or "correct" agency is a complete subjective decision made by the designers of SIMSI. As mentioned above, case summaries are provided to the Initiating Agents.

FIGURE 2

Case____________________

TREATMENT PLAN USED IN SIMSI

Page_____

Problem	Service Required	Agency	Appointment Date & Time	Comments

These summaries were written with specific services and specific agencies predetermined as appropriate or "correct." These subjective decisions provide an objective measurement of effectiveness for the purposes of the simulation. Effectiveness, is measured in percentage points: thus, a treatment plan can be 20 percent, 80 percent, etc., "correct."

Phase II of SIMSI utilizes the same case summaries, the same methods of evaluation, but introduces a team approach to treatment planning and a computer. A computer was used, figuratively rather than literally, by means of a simple data processing system called Indecks.[5] This is commercially available and is actually a series of prepunched cards which can be written on and accessed according to an almost limitless number of variables.

The dramatic change during Phase II concerns philosophy and process. There exists a federal and community commitment to integration of services. This commitment is operationalized in a central assessment and referral agency through which all clients are channeled. The process differs by the use of a team of human service workers to plan for client needs aided by a computer-based information and referral system. The 20 players of Phase I are now divided into five teams, use the same cases, and are evaluated by the same criteria of efficiency and effectiveness. (See Figure 3.) In Phase II the "computer" is able to provide information on what services are available in the community and actually make an appointment for a client with a specific agency.

A simulation or game at any significant level of sophistication demands that extraneous variables or contingencies be designed in to affect the outcome. These should be contingencies that the players exercise no control over at all. In simulation and gaming literature this is called the "roll of the dice" input--that chance occurrence no one expects to happen but

FIGURE 3

PHYSICAL ARRANGEMENT OF PLAYERS DURING PHASE II

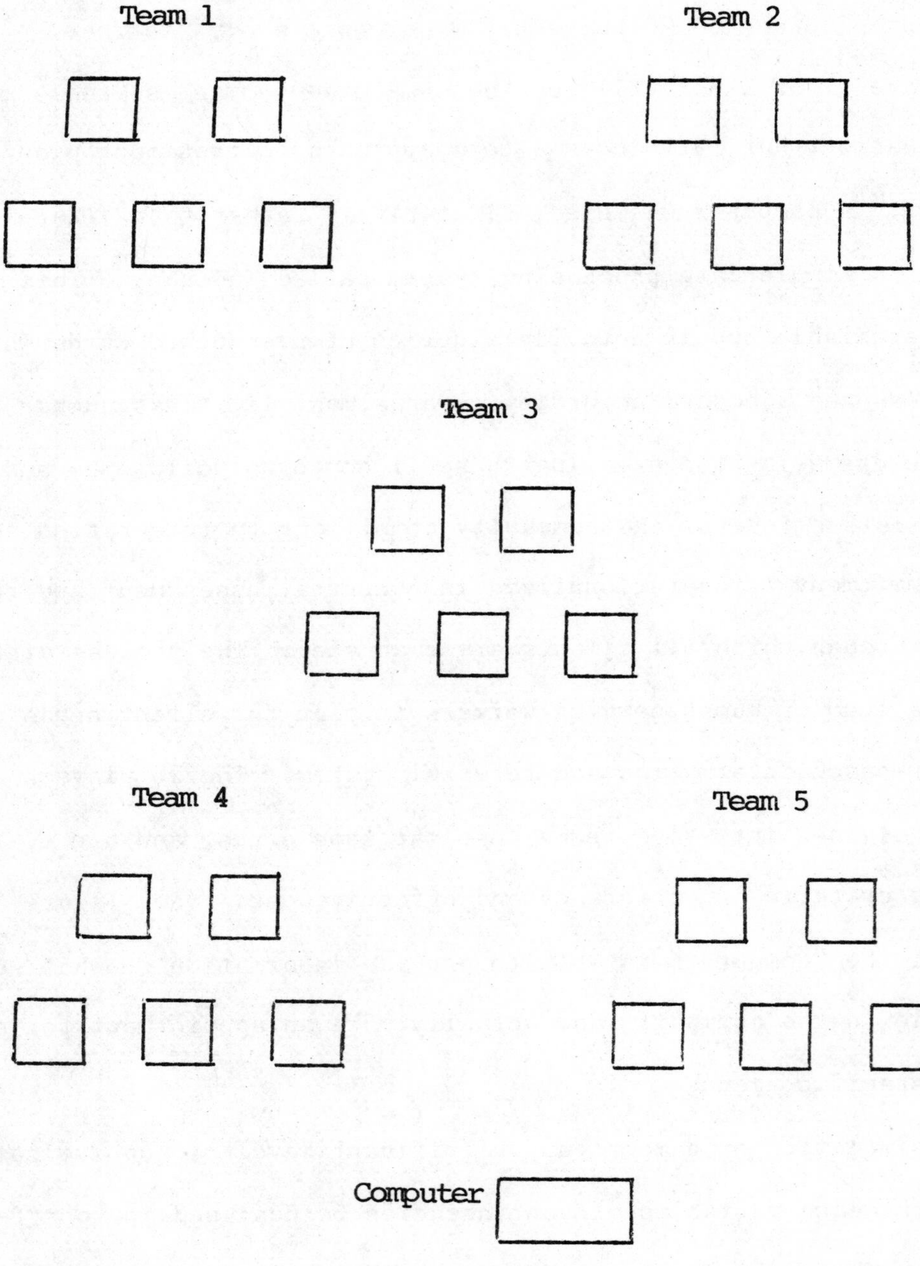

Team 1

Team 2

Team 3

Team 4

Team 5

Computer

which inevitably does as in real-life situations. In SIMSI, these extraneous variables are called contingency cards and influence players during both phases of the simulation. Examples of contingency cards which are introduced regularly during the interactions are:

> "You have an emergency call on another line--you are unavailable for the next two minutes."

> "The computer is down for the next four minutes."

Preliminary Results

The hypothesis tested is that Phase II of the experience--emphasizing a computer assisted central intake and referral center--would be both more effective and efficient than present operations as simulated in Phase I. As state above, efficiency was gauged by the time measured in minutes it took to complete a treatment plan, and effectiveness was gauged by the percent of "correct" parts of the treatment plan.

The preliminary results are both disappointing because of a failure to prove positively our hypothesis and also challenging because of several serendipitous, unanticipated findings. The quantitative data from the preliminary exercise of SIMSI are shown in Figure 4.

Several factors can explain the less than favorable results, particularly in terms of the efficiency ratings. A technical difficulty encountered during the preliminary testing was the physical inaccessibility of the "computer" to the players. The computer--the Indecks data retrieval system-- was capable of delivering the information, but the human element failed. Simply stated, we had one computer terminal attempting to serve 20 players at the same time. The obvious remedy for this problem is to multiply the "computer" by five so that during Phase II each treatment planning team will have access to its own terminal. Not only did the presence of only one terminal decrease efficiency, literally making people line up in front

FIGURE 4

Case	Effectiveness (percent)		Effectiveness (percent)	
	Phase I	Phase II	Phase I	Phase II
Vines	60	40	71.02	78.18
Martin	40	20	68.40	66.44
Thomas	40	40	60.15	56.22
Randall	30	50	48.41	65.22
Brown	70	80	44.27	69.04
	$\overline{X}$ =48 SD =50.1	$\overline{X}$ =46 SD=50	$\sum$ =292.25 $\overline{X}$ = 58. SD= 59.40	$\sum$ =335.10 $\overline{X}$ = 67. SD= 67.39

of the computer and thereby wasting time, it also unwittingly dissolved the treatment teams, who were by design supposed to be planning as a group.

Even in the face of these technical problems, which are being corrected in 40 percent of the cases (the Martin and Thomas cases), Phase II was more efficient. The overall average efficiency, however, is less for Phase II (58.4 minutes for Phase I, 67 minutes for Phase II).

In analyzing the raw data for effectiveness, it was apparent that one team--those planning for the Martin case--had misunderstood the instructions and therefore did not complete the treatment plan as indicated. Thus, the very low effectiveness score of 20 percent for the Martin case negatively skewed the entire effectiveness average for Phase II. In spite of this factor, however, it is apparent that in 60 percent of the cases (Thomas, Randall, and Brown), the effectiveness rating was higher than, or at least the same as, Phase I.

These are preliminary results subject to modification as SIMSI is developed and refined further.

Projections for the Future

As mentioned earlier in this paper, SIMSI was one component of a federal grant to the College of Public and Community Services at the University of Missouri - Columbia. The seminal focus of the grant and of SIMSI was training of human service professionals within an integrated context of practice and organization. The participants in the preliminary testing of SIMSI were social workers, recreational therapists and community developers. The immediate phenomenon that emerged during Phase II, when a team rather than an individual planned for the client, were major philosophical differences to the task of problem definition and service determination. Thus, there existed conceptual differences in the way a social worker and a community developer viewed the multiproblem family. It was not the expected difference of casework versus community organization but rather whether advocacy was needed for a particular family or for the entire neighborhood. Even within a profession all was not tranquil and calm. Social workers argued among themselves whether alcoholism was the signal problem or only a symptom, whether in-patient was more beneficial than outpatient services, and whether individual or group counseling was indicated as the treatment of choice.

What evolved then was a new research question: is a human service professional's treatment philosophy the most critical variable in determining how he or she integrates human services? Perhaps, then, it is not so much one's professional training or socialization, or the territoriality created and defended by agencies and institutions that is foremost in determining whether truly integrated services are possible or not, but rather the individual, intricate composite of training, personality and environment called one's own treatment philosophy. If it is true that there is "something" beyond one's own professional discipline or beyond one's own agency or institution, then we trainers, whether in universities or in human service agencies, must face it squarely. It argues for a more affective rather than cognitive approach to interprofessional training so that the trainees or students, whatever their role is, do not develop a limited, sterile, myopic treatment philosophy.

I will close at this point with some random and severely underdeveloped thoughts for further refinement of SIMSI and for further use of the methodology of simulation/gaming. One approach would be to computerize the entire process of SIMSI this time with actual, not simulated computers. A

computerized system would allow individuals and small groups to "play" the
game or "experience" the simulation without the necessity of composing a
group of 20 at one time, which is a continual and perplexing problem.
Computerization would also allow for more consistent and reliable evaluative
data since the entire process would be more formalized by the very nature
of its being stored in the data banks of a computer.

A radically different approach would be to expand both the time factor
and the environment of the simulation by creating an entire human service
agency. This is not science fiction but is entirely within the realm of
possibility. There is, for example, at least one law school that I am
aware of, the University of New York at Buffalo, that utilizes a simulated
law firm for teaching purposes. A simulated social service agency has
fascinating possibilities, I believe, for the training of new professionals
and for the continuing training of those already struggling against pervasive
social problems.

One concluding word about simulation as a method of training and
education: it occupies a midpoint on the continuum of classroom to real
life agency experience. That is both its strength and its weakness.
Simulation is never truly real, but it certainly can be more real and
interesting than the lecture or discussion method of the classroom or staff
training center. If the Department of the Defense can play war games,
apparently successfully, I fail to perceive why human service professionals
should be ashamed to play similar games for a more noble purpose: the
eradication of social problems. Simulations will never solve those problems,
but they can train in an effective and humanistic manner those who will
plan and intervene and, it is hoped, succeed.

FOOTNOTES

1. C. Greenblat, "Simulations, Games and the Sociologist," _American Sociologist_, Vol. 6, 1971, p. 161.

2. C. Abt, "Games for Learning" in _Simulation Games in Learning_, S. Babcock and E. Schild, editors (Beverly Hills: Sage Publications, 1968), p. 72.

3. D. Harper and H. C. Selvin, "Computer Simulation and the Teaching of Research Methods," _American Sociologist_, Vol. 8, 1973, p. 64.

4. R. Glazier, _How To Design Educational Games_ (Cambridge: Abt Associates, 1971).

5. _Research Deck_ (Arlington, Vermont: Indecks Company, 1966).

6. P. Hollander, "The Use of Simulation in Teaching Law and Lawyering Skills," _Simulation and Games_, Vol. 8, No. 3, 1977.

IV. The Implementation of Training Processes

In this section on implementation of the training process, Diane Piktialis presents a case study of a project by the Massachusetts State Agency on Aging to organize the educational programs from several different universities and colleges to meet the training needs of local human service agencies in the field of aging. This study describes how the use of training monies and the contracting process enabled the state agency to involve substate area agencies on aging and local service providers in planning the training process with both public and private educational institutions.

The paper describes in some detail the formation of the state training committee composed of consumers of training; the use of research fund proposals within the state to specify the parameters of training needs; and the building of training consortia at the regional level composed of educational institutions and service providers to engage in local training needs assessment and training resource identification and modification. Piktialis closes with a discussion of the potential application of this approach to the major service/training areas such as Title XX.

Planning a Statewide Training Network: A Case Study in Developing Interorganizational Relationships

by Diane S. Piktialis

Diane S. Piktialis, Ph.D., is Chief Planner in Education for the Commonwealth of Massachusetts Department of Elder Affairs.

A number of social changes are creating a favorable environment for educational institutions to develop nontraditional training programs in the field of aging. The large and rapidly growing number of older Americans has recently stimulated the efforts of state and federal governments to develop service programs for the elderly.[1] In the past six years, agencies have focused on immediate necessities such as planning, establishing program structure, and determining eligibility criteria. Program development and expanding services for the growing elderly population have also created a need for trained manpower to provide services. Staff development and in-service training are now pressing concerns.[2]

Agencies serving the elderly, such as area agencies on aging and home care corporations; frequently utilize underdeveloped manpower. Advisory boards often consist of lay community members who serve voluntarily; direct service staff are often college graduates without professional training. Development of basic social service and outreach skills is imperative in the achievement of quality care and standards of performance. Skill training within the framework of general knowledge of gerontology is a must for persons working with the elderly and their families. Moreover, the need

for training is slowly becoming recognized by policy makers, administrators,

and practitioners in many other areas of human services.[3]

Paralleling recognition of the need for training has been a change in

facts and assumptions directing public policy in higher education. A

recent paper distributed by the Secretary of Education in Massachusetts

noted that patterns of population growth in the last two decades will not

continue.[4] In the next two decades, the Commonwealth's institutions will

feel the impact of two fundamental shifts in the age composition of the

population of Massachusetts: The 18-21 year old age group will decline

substantially and the 24-44 year old population will increase.

The most probable result of these population shifts which parallel

national trends will be a significant decline in full-time undergraduate

student demand and enrollments by traditional college age population. Yet,

these demographic changes also produce an opportunity to meet a previously

unfulfilled demand--namely, increased service through full-time, part-time,

and continuing education for the growing adult population.

Finally, policy makers in the field of educational gerontology have

noted the potential training role for higher learning institutions. In his

dicussion of the state of the art, David A. Peterson has suggested several

roles for higher education. Among these are education for the elderly and

about aging, and continuing and in-service education for practitioners to

upgrade their service potential and to attract new workers into the field

(through education and preservice training programs.)[5]

Thus, several factors--training needs in human services and gerontology,

the needs of educational institutions to recruit new student groups to

offset declining enrollments, and a desire to relate more closely to the

needs of their community--have combined to provide a favorable atmosphere
for attempting to create nontraditional programs that will relate more
closely to the needs of a changing clientele. A major objective of these
efforts should be development of educational and training programs to
bridge the gap between the acquisition of knowledge and the application of
that knowledge in the delivery of service and the development of policy.

The Problem

While the time is ripe for educational institutions to provide training
to individuals in the field of aging, organizational development in Western
society has inhibited interaction between the institutions of education and
human service organizations.

Those living in the twentieth century have witnessed the accelerated
growth and expansion of large organizations. One dimension commonly shared
by modern organizations is their division of labor. Another feature of
these organizational patterns which is taken for granted is increasing
specialization.[6] While these organizational patterns have been described
at length for large corporations, several features of the corporate economy,
such as segmentation and specialization, have been developing in service
organizations as well. One often hears practitioners criticize academic
institutions as being ivory towers and out of touch with reality. This
view of education, expressed in everyday cliches by people in the "real
worlds" of business, industry and government, indicates a commonplace
perception of organizational automony and a concomitant distrust of academe.

Rigid separation of functions in different types of organizations is
an important obstacle in launching, directing, and coordinating broadbased
training programs. My own experience in both higher education and training

in the human services has substantiated this widespread split. On the one hand, academics who claim to know the latest research and to be able to relate to practitioners often revert to questions of how they can become more practical and relate to the community during planning discussions. On the other hand, practitioners speak of the training capacity of traditional educators with great reservation, wondering whether they can provide meaningful training related to practical job realities instead of just "pie in the sky" ideas.

This paper will discuss and analyze a case study of a project to merge education and human services in order to develop training programs. The study was of a statewide project administered by the State Agency on Aging, designed to meet training needs by interfacing training and institutions of higher education with human service agencies in the field of aging. At the same time, the hidden objective of the project was to build a long-term training and gerontological capacity in public educational institutions in the state.

THE STUDY

The study describes and analyzes a two-year effort by the Massachusetts Department of Elder Affairs to plan and develop a statewide training network to provide quality training to practitioners in the field of gerontology. Through the use of Title IV-A training monies and the planning and contracting process, the State Agency was able to involve substate planning and service areas (including local service providers) directly in the planning process with public, and eventually private, educational institutions.

Background and History

In 1974-75, the first year of Administration on Aging training support, the entire amount of Title IV-A funds was subgranted to the Executive Office of Educational Affairs and then subgranted to community colleges and other educational resources. Ten subcontracts were let, totalling $78,896. Nine hundred and seventy-four persons, 57 percent of whom were elders, received training in advocacy, community organization, program development and management, and the aging process. Although the target population was appropriately reached and costs for the program were well within the initial guidelines, two problem areas were identified.

First, by subcontracting the total amount of funds, the Department of Education did not provide sufficient staff for day-to-day monitoring of the program. This resulted in reporting and fiscal inefficiencies, and hindered the impact on the community college system. The second problem area was the emphasis on continuing education divisions of the state colleges, rather than on the regular day divisions. Thus, the programs were not incorporated into the regular course curriculum and college administration, and no mechanism was developed for continuing gerontological activities at the removal of Office of Educational Affairs funding support.

In 1975, attempts were made to correct these deficiencies by developing a staff position in the Department of Elder Affairs. The Chief Planner in Education had the responsibility for managing the Title IV-A program in DEA.[7] His role was to stimulate educational activities for and about elders in two and four-year public colleges throughout the state, and to coordinate Title IV-A activities with the other training activities of DEA.[8] The development of this new DEA staff position proved profitable in correcting the deficiencies of the previous year's program. The Chief

Planner, with the assistance of two student interns, was able to implement monitoring procedures, to identify administrative and fiscal problems at individual colleges and to offer the expertise and support needed to remedy potential and/or real problems.

The Department's policy during this first year was to use Title IV-A funds as seed money and as the first step to institutionalized support for training and education in aging. The Chief Planner at that time was on leave from a community college. He was knowledgable about the state system of higher education, and this enabled him to develop a communications network between DEA and each college as well as between colleges themselves. This greatly increased the impact of DEA on the state college system. Through outreach and the development of ongoing relationships with college presidents and academic deans, the Chief Planner increased awareness of DEA programs and activities, particularly in the area of educational programs. In addition, college presidents and academic deans were encouraged to incorporate gerontological curricula within the regularly state-funded academic activities of the colleges and not in continuing education divisions. This provided better opportunities for regular students to be exposed to aging and elders, and for elders to be exposed to community colleges and state universities. It also increased the integration of gerontological course content and elders into the college system, and created the mechanism for continued state funding of the gerontological activities.

Raising the Consciousness of Higher Education: The Beginning of Capacity Building

Twenty-seven institutions were contacted by DEA regarding the goals and objectives of Title IV-A programs for 1976. At this time, the Chief Planner was engaged in vigorous outreach at the colleges, visiting many public institutions in the State. Other colleges were telephoned following the initial visits in order to stimulate the interest of college presidents, dean of faculty, and continuing education departments in developing programs for older people and for those working with older people.

Proposals were due at DEA in February. Nineteen institutions drafted proposals, which included details of project goals and objectives for 1976, a description of prior college activities in gerontology, vitae of project directors, and budget requests. The Chief Planner and the interns reviewed the proposals, and made recommendations for funding. Seventeen institutions were funded at this time.

The Programs

A wide variety of projects was funded by Title IV-A at the seventeen institutions. Activities included seminars for elders and those working with elders in advocacy techniques and the aging process; development of gerontological curriculum, to be included in full-time degree programs; faculty training in gerontology; seminars for full-time students in gerontology; one-day conferences on aging and available resources, which were attended by elders, faculty members, students, community members, and practitioners; transportation to educational programs for elders and the handicapped; scholarships for elders to take regular college courses for credit. The events took place during April, May and June and were held throughout the state at community and four-year colleges and other local centers. Most programs during this period were intended to raise consciousness for and about aging rathern than to provide skills training.

Some of the colleges exhibited many administrative strengths during the development of their projects. Those who had the support of higher administrators, including the college presidents, deans of faculty, and deans of continuing education, were able to administer their projects better than those college administrators who were indifferent to the Title IV-A programs. Western Community College[9] was one institution which began its involvement in gerontology with the Title IV-A grant and was able to draw 160 participants to its event, with the extensive support of the dean of faculty. Commonwealth Community College, on the other hand, floundered initially while attempting to establish its programs. Its dean of faculty appeared to lack interest in assisting the college to become more directed in its educational pursuits for older people.

Those colleges which oriented more to working with their community members and to doing extensive outreach to stimulate the interest of the elderly, demonstrated more administrative direction. West Suburban Community College exemplifies this in its extensive work to cultivate interest within the community and to bring in older people. Countless visits to local organizations resulted in 299 attendees, who are enthusiastically requesting future involvement with the college.

Development of ongoing relationships with community college presidents and academic deans was viewed as an important factor in creating a network among academic institutions. Constant communication was established between the State Agency and project directors at the colleges. The overall effect was to establish administrative support for the programs and to begin to develop a mechanism of accountability from the grantees.[10] Also a communications network was started throughout the state, through which personnel at one institution could be informed of the efforts, activities, and resources of those at other institutions. For many directors, this was the first time they were put in direct communication with those who shared their commitments to gerontology.

The actual leadership role played by the State Unit on Aging proved effective in alerting institutions to their obligations to the changing populations. The result was to improve the program planning and proposal design in accordance with the educational needs of older people. The State Unit also stimulated commitments to this target population in an ongoing way. The programs which the Chief Planner encouraged in his personal contact with colleges proved to be greatly diversified and creative, indicating the value of explicitly conveying to the colleges what should be done regarding older people.

Thus, many activities engaged in by the State Unit on Aging laid the groundwork for developing a statewide training network among public institutions of higher education. By using seed funds to begin gerontology programs, the Department of Elder Affairs exercised strong leadership in the development and coordination of education and a few training activities for elders and agencies serving elders. During the first year, the Title IV-A program was successful in generating considerable interest in state colleges, community colleges and public universities, and contributed to developing the capacity of those institutions to deliver such training. In short, the strategy of giving centralized direction to a statewide program was successful in making many institutions of higher education more aware of and interested in gerontology.

Building the Network

In the initial year just described, the state agency focused on the educational aspect of building a statewide network, because federal and state program objectives making institutions of higher learning more sensitive to the need for building programs in gerontology. This section discusses the human service aspect, specifically, the problem of getting planning input and program participation from most human service agencies.

Largely because of changes in federal regulations, the second year's focus shifted significantly as the needs of practitioners changed. The objective was to deliver advanced education and skill training to agencies serving elders and to those elders interested in training in aging. The new training focus required a more systematic way of assessing training needs and establishing priorities.

In order to obtain a systematic and accurate estimate of local and state training needs and priorities, the State Agency contracted for an assessment of training needs in Massachusetts and an identification of training priorities by local program directors. Based on that report, a training plan was developed and an invitation for proposals (RFP) sent to all public institutions of higher education.[11] The policy of subgranting only to public institutions of higher education was maintained because of limited funds and a desire to continue to build programs in the public sector. Unlike the first year, funding was provided for actual training activities rather than for consciousness-raising types of activities were replaced. At the same time, planning continued to address ways in which a network could be established to deliver training. The most important component of this planning strategy was to develop joint planning with aging agencies around training objectives at the state and substate level.

The first step in joint planning was formation of a State Training Committee to advise in the implementation of Title IV-A training activities for the 1977 fiscal year and to begin development of long-range training objectives. The training committee was made up of delegates from the state

agency; local agencies, including area agencies on aging, home care corporations, and Title VII nutrition projects; and educators with reputations in
gerontology. The committee met bimonthly during the year to discuss broad
issues, such as evaluation of current programs and identification of training
gaps and priorities for the next year's training plan. Several members
served as liaisons representing state associations or various types of
agencies. In addition, the new Chief Planner regularly met with an Education Committee of the Nutrition Project Directors Association.

In order to cultivate the trust of agencies in these processes, the
Department of Elder Affairs contracted for an independent evaluation of
Title IV-A training programs delivered by the various colleges and universities.
Results of those evaluations were later made available to area agencies
before the start of fall 1977 programs in order to aid agency personnel in
the selection of appropriate training.

As before, the Department of Elder Affairs played a pivotal role in
its attempts to develop a creative and productive partnership between
educational institutions and network agencies for the delivery of appropriate
training in Massachusetts. The Department found it necessary to take major
steps to work cooperatively with aging agencies in order to develop and
implement training programs that would address their priority needs. More
importantly, extensive agency input was needed to establish the trust
necessary for developing relationships between those agencies and colleges.

Representation at the substate level was built in through the RFP
process and through conditions of all training grant awards. All proposals
for Title IV-A funds were required to have a letter of support from the
appropriate area agency or, in the case of an undesignated area, the local
home care corporation. Also, each Notification of Grant Award required

formation of an advisory committee representing the appropriate area agency and other aging agencies and postsecondary educational institutions at the local level.

The Department plans to continue to exercise strong leadership in the development of training for elders and agencies serving elders through joint planning with area agencies on aging home care corporations, and through Title VII projects based on training objectives. A new and major component of those plans is to develop regional consortiums of educational institutions and aging agencies which will have two roles: (1) training needs assessment by agencies; and (2) resource identifiction and mobilization by the colleges. Five such consortiums have met at least once prior to the last RFP cycle.[12] By developing these regional consortiums into working groups, much of the needs assessment, planning, and recruitment can be accomplished at the local or regional level. The Department intends to act as a facilitator to formalize these groups into regional working consortiums, and ultimately to move toward joint submission of grant proposals by an educational institution and aging agency (or agencies).

In sum, state agency contracting focuses on education institutions and uses clearly defined behavioral objectives to identify potential program needs. Integration of planning, contracting, and service delivery through this system results in an organizational base for ongoing training and educational programs in aging. That base consists of links between the aging network and the education institutions, and between colleges and universities and local communities.

CONCLUSIONS

Efforts to develop a statewide aging training network were based on analysis of the tasks performed in rendering services to the aged, and the specific skills, knowledge, and attitudes needed by service providers and identification of educational resources that could contribute to the development of these training components.

In order to bridge the gap between the acquisition and application of knowledge in the delivery of services and the development of policy, it was necessary to create not only a traditional academic core curriculum of biology, psychology, and sociology of aging, but also to include practical field experiences and other training methods directly related to job skills. This required a redirection of educational philosophy and selection of training models which would be adapted to the immediate needs of different groups of practitioners.

In early stages of the program, most of the in-class formal training was generally limited to the aging process and the characteristics of the elderly. Courses that focused on the techniques of working specifically with older adults and on community resources for the elderly were few. The evaluation responses seemed to stress that while the liberal arts were a good base, the participants would like to see more of the practical arts.

Such responses caused a redirection of the Title IV-A training program. Early conferences, institutes, and seminars of a consciousness-raising type were largely replaced with skill training and skill related knowledge and opportunities for practice. Trainers were encouraged to have their programs based in agencies and, where possible, to support the learning-by-doing techniques which have proven successful in adult training. Early seed monies and capacity building laid the groundwork and established educator-practitioner relationships that enable program redirection and increased ability to deliver training statewide.

The institutional impact of the Title IV-A program was as important in developing an aging network as the programmatic aspects of curriculum development and training content, though the two developed side by side. The institutional impact can be divided into four areas: (1) development of a contracting process for Title IV-A funds with clear, measurable objectives to assure accountability; (2) expansion of resources for the Aging Network through educational institutions; (3) attentiveness to meeting generic skill needs and human service needs for the Aging Network; and (4) development of a growing collaborative planning and training base.

Though the Department of Elder Affairs is far from being able to meet all training needs through this developing network, much of its success to date can be traced to the strengths of centralized planning and administration. DEA's central role in managing training brought a statewide perspective to planning, needs assessment, and resource identification. Leadership provided by the State Agency and the Chief Planner allowed development of ongoing relationships with the community, state college presidents and academic deans. Outreach activities generated greater diversity in locations and programs; improved program planning and proposal design, and increased community awareness for elders and aging. In the final analysis, however, success of this training program is due to collaborative efforts involving the participation of the state agency on aging, area agencies on aging home care corporations, nutrition projects, and the educational community.

Service agency collaboration has also had the unintended consequence of opening channels of communication often severed through political conflict and competition on the local level for a greater share of service dollars. Many training programs found that when personnel from the home care corporations, Title VII nutrition projects, area agencies on aging, councils on aging, and other agencies, intermingled in training courses, ideas were freely exchanged and participants gained new respect for each other.

Although this paper has focused largely on successes, there were many localities where there was no trust and collaboration and an effective training base did not develop. Clearly, much is to be learned in this area and controlled attempts to train and evaluate are sorely needed.

IMPLICATIONS

Although this study describes only the training program of the State Agency on Aging, its progress and successes suggest its applicability to training in other substantive areas in state government and human services.

The Commonwealth of Massachusetts currently has a Task Force on Title XX Training and Retraining comprised of policy-level representatives of all human service agencies in the State of Massachusetts which currently provide services under Title XX.[13] The Task Force has been a working group since October 1976 and was responsible for the Massachusetts Title XX Training/Retraining Plan. The Plan was the result of a year-long collaborative planning effort involving representatives from each State Human Service Agency.[14]

The strategy of the Task Force was to begin to develop the capacity of higher educational resources in the State to provide quality training to staff of all human service agencies, as well as to contracted providers. As stated in the Training/Retraining Plan, Massachusetts' approach to training, for the most part, and at least for 1978 fiscal year, emphasizes:

> "...using the capabilities of the Commonwealth's university
> and college system but focusing attention on meeting the
> short-term training needs of the social service system. For
> this reason, much of the training will involve the development
> of courses which are at least partially new, responding to the
> requirements defined by this Plan (and by supporting requests
> for proposals), rather than simply buying space in existing
> courses for Title XX staff.[15]

Implementation of the Title XX training project will provide a case study with which to test the applicability of the model of aging training network development, structure, and processes presented in this paper to the wider field of human services.

FOOTNOTES

1. The Federal Government became a focal point in providing leadership and services for the elderly with the passage of the Older Americans Act in 1965. The Act created the Administration on Aging as an operating agency within HEW. The White House Conference on Aging in 1971 was also instrumental in recommending expansion of federal service dollars allocated to the elderly.

2. To achieve this goal, the Administration on Aging makes Title IV-A funds available to State Agencies on Aging for the purpose of strengthening their responsiveness to the need for more adequately trained personnel in the field of aging and by meeting priority in-service training needs at the state and area levels for individuals currently providing services to the elderly.

3. An example of this growing concern is Title XX of the Social Security Act which now provides reimbursement to the states for a wide range of training and retraining activities. These funds are intended to develop a pool of qualified workers who provide social services under each state's Title XX program.

4. Commonwealth of Massachusetts, Executive Office of Educational Affairs, Working Paper on Public Higher Education Planning, August 1977.

5. David A. Peterson, "The State of the Act," Educational Gerontology, Vol. 1, No. 1 (January-March 1976), pp. 61-75.

6. Amitai Etzioni, Modern Organizations (Englewood Cliffs, N.J.: Prentice Hall, Inc., 1964); and Robert Prethus, The Organization Society (New York: Vantage Books, 1965).

7. DEA is an abbreviation for Department of Elder Affairs.

8. The Fiscal Year 1976 Title IV-A program was designed to provide educational opportunities for elders.

   Specifically, the five objectives of the program were:

   a. To provide educational opportunities to elders to assist them in taking an active and effective part in social and programmatic decisions that affect their lives.

   b. To provide education and training opportunities to elders and persons working with elders to assist them in becoming more effective in providing services to elders.

   c. To stimulate among the students of post-secondary educational institutions a concern for elders, knowledge about aging, and an interest in working with elders.

d. To work towards making education for and about elders an integral part of the educational process in institutions of higher learning.

e. To develop in the Department of Elder Affairs a capacity to coordinate educational and training activities for elders.

9. This name and the name of all other colleges have been changed to disguise the sources.

10. Grantee accountability is a critical problem in the early stages of program development and is especially important in the area of training in human services where proven evaluation methods and established standards of performance are lacking.

11. The Title IV-A program for Fiscal Year 1977 was designed to provide training and education for staff of agencies working with the Department of Elder Affairs including Area Agencies on Aging, Home Care Corporations, and Title VII Nutrition Projects. Specifically the four objectives as contained in the RFP were:

a. To provide information in techniques of monitoring and evaluation in selected staff of agencies working with the Department of Elder Affairs.

Monitoring of programs operations and evaluation of program effectiveness are critical to the management of services to elders. Training in the techniques of monitoring and evaluation should focus on:

--Establishing measurable objectives and performance criteria;

--Designing monitoring and evaluation instruments and data collection procedures;

--Involving consumers in the evaluation process;

--Developing strategies for translating the results of monitoring and evaluation into effective programs for action.

b. To provide information on techniques of program development, program management, and related job skills to selected staff of agencies working with DEA. Training content should focus on:

--Budgeting grant and contract development;

--Grant and contract management;

--Social service delivery skills, such as outreach, assessment, service planning, and case management.

c. To provide instruction in the principles of Social Gerontology to selected staff of agencies working with elders.

Agencies serving elders need basic information on elders and the aging process to upgrade the quality of services to elders. The content of social gerontology courses should include attitudes on aging, the sociology of aging, the psychology of aging, the economics of aging, and techniques for working with elders.

d. To provide information on programs and services for elders to selected staff members of all categories of agencies serving elders.

Training should be provided in one or more of the following content areas:

--Income and health maintenance programs;

--Housing and community development programs;

--Transportation services;

--Preretirement planning;

--Social services, with an emphasis on services designed to alleviate isolation and increase social participation;

--Consumer services.

12. Of five regional groups of human service agencies and educational institutions only two have been successful in terms of ongoing planning and cooperation. The other three met only around the time of the RFP process to reduce competitive proposal bidding.

13. Title XX of the Social Security Act provides federal reimbursement to the states for a wide range of social services. States participating in the Title XX program are required to undertake comprehensive planning for social services, monitor and evaluate social service delivery, and establish standards for program quality. The complexity of the Title XX program requires new kinds of administrative and service delivery skills to ensure effective implementation of the State's Plan. To encourage and support the development of these needed skills, Title XX authorizes federal funds for the training and re-training of those personnel who plan, deliver, and administer social services under the state's Title XX program.

14. The state human service agencies currently providing services under Title XX are:

Department of Public Welfare
Massachusetts Commission for the Blind
Department of Mental Health
Office for Children

Department of Youth Services
Department of Corrections
Department of Public Health
Massachusetts Rehabilitation Commission
Department of Elder Affairs

The Executive Office of Human Services Task Force on Training and Retraining, consisting of policy-level representatives of each of the
above agencies, met approximately twice a month from July 1976 through
October 1977. The primary objectives of this group were to review the
many possible options for training/retraining programs under Title XX,
to develop a consensus on strategy for providing the training, and to
define a limited number of training objectives based on the indicated
training needs of the participating agencies. Working within this
policy framework, the Title XX Planning Staff and Training Unit in the
Department of Public Welfare developed the body of the plan for review
and approval by the Task Force.

15. <u>Massachusetts Title XX Training and Retraining Plan</u>, 1977, p. 4.

BIBLIOGRAPHY

Commonwealth of Massachusetts, Department of Public Welfare. Social Services Training and Retraining Plan. Amendment to the Title XX Comprehensive Social Service Plan. Boston: Fiscal Year 1978.

Commonwealth of Massachusetts, Executive Office of Educational Affairs. Working Paper on Public Higher Education Planning. Boston: August 1977.

Ehrlich, Ira F., and Phyllis D. Ehrlich. "A Four-Part Framework to Meet the Responsibilities of Higher Education to Gerontology," Educational Gerontology, Vol. 1, No. 3 (July-September 1976), pp. 251-261.

Etzioni, Amitai. Modern Organizations. Englewood Cliffs, New Jersey: Prentice-Hall, Inc., 1964.

Peterson, David A. "The State of the Art." Educational Gerontology, Vol. 1; No. 1; January-March 1976, pp. 61-75.

Prethus, Robert. The Organization Society. New York: Vantage Books, 1965.

White, Sally, Dennis Hameister, and Tom Hickey. Community Based Training: A Model for University and State Partnerships in Topical Papers. Series 1, Educational Programming and Community Research in Gerontology. Gerontology Center, Amy Gardner House, Pennsylvania State University, University Park, Pennsylvania.

V.   The Implementation of Training Techniques

This final section includes three papers which address the actual implementation of training in three widely different settings. Diane Stagliano discusses the implementation of interviewing training for public assistance workers using an androgogical approach. She assesses the relationship of management style and organizational millieu in the implementation of such a training approach. Judson Morris describes the provision of training to residents and staff of a mental health half-way house in a joint training group. He also deals with the relationship of those in positions of authority to the nature of training and how training can provide a threat to those in control. Finally, Gemma Beckley and Gary Mooers describe a program of helping nursing home administrators gain a better understanding of social work and social services through a specialized training program.

Stagliano discusses the application of an andragogical approach to the development and provision of interviewing training to public assistance workers in the state of New Jersey. This approach involves the analysis of organizational goals. She discusses the problems posed by the current political climate in public welfare. The emphasis on quantification as the only measure of accountability in public assistance and the nature of the motivation of staff entering public assistance. She describes how the androgogical approach can facilitate development of employees who are competent, efficient, effective and humane in client contacts.

Morris describes an approach to mental health training which involved training residents and staff at a half-way house together in one group. Although staff members were provided some initial training in intervention modalities, both staff and residents engaged in a series of training exercises related to communication and mental health intervention. Such areas as behavior modification, contracting, token economics and problem solving were covered. Morris analyzes the impact of carrying out this type of joint training, especially as it affects the total life of the resident unit. He describes the differential impacts on staff and residents and the potential stress it created when residents wanted to take more responsibility for themselves.

Beckley and Mooers describe the development and provision of training to acquaint nursing home administrators with the profession of social work and to show the potential value of social services in the nursing home setting. Sessions covering the social work profession, needs of nursing home patients and their families, the social worker in the nursing home setting, setting priorities in nursing homes and common problems in nursing home social work are described in some detail.

An Andragogical Approach to Assistance Payments Interviewer Training

by Diane M. Stagliano

Diane M. Stagliano, M.S.W., is Chief Training Officer of the New Jersey Division of Public Welfare.

In 1975 in response to much concern about the quality of interviewer skills for assistance payments in New Jersey County Welfare Agencies, the Division of Public Welfare Staff Development and Training Unit began engaging county assistance payments trainers in an organizational development process which focused on interviewer training. This process was pursued because New Jersey has a state-supervised, county-administered welfare system which means that there are major structural differences between the 21 county agencies as well as major differences in skill levels between county trainers. Consequently, flexibility had to be incorporated in the training which would allow for these differences.

As a result of trainer and trainee needs being identified during this process, a collection of structured learning experiences sequenced for the training of interviewing skills to new CWA assistance payments workers was developed. This "Interviewing Training Module" is designed for use by assistance payments trainers of varying skill levels. It is organized into four major sections: (1) Introductions to Interviewing; (2) Facts, Inferences, and Assumptions--Observation and Listening Skills; (3) Interviewing Skills;

and (4) Interview Concerns, Principles, and Ethics. Within each section, objectives, aids, materials, techniques, and references are discussed.

The structured experiences range from perceptual and frame of reference exercises to structured role-play, skill-practice activities. Trainer theory, instructions for each experience, processing information, and lecturettes are provided and thoroughly discussed. This results in a collection of generic interview training material that is specifically oriented to assistance payments tasks. This collection can be adapted or selectively used as the needs of the trainees warrant and the skills of the trainer permit. The major difference between this and other interview training designs is that this represents an andragogical approach to training rather than a content approach and is based on an andragogical design model which is a process model.

This approach attempts to recognize fully the needs of the adult learner as being different from those of children (andragogy versus pedagogy). The units of experiential learning are sequenced and structured around problem areas the adult trainees are assisted in identifying. Formats and appropriate materials and methods are selected and arranged according to trainee needs and learning readiness.

Although what has been discussed thus far may not seem revolutionary, it is certainly a departure from traditional content training where outcomes, content, methods, etc., are planned ahead without considering the learner's needs or desires. Because however, many agencies expect traditional content training, the factors around the decision to pursue this kind of approach should be carefully analyzed. Some of the considerations useful in arriving at such a decision can be organized around three areas: the trainee target, the organization, and society. Public Welfare and particularly the assistance payments function presents peculiar dilemmas in the use of such an approach.

An andragogical approach is based on certain theories and assumptions. The assumptions of andragogy vs. pedagogy as summarized by Malcolm Knowles[3] are as follows:

ASSUMPTIONS

	Pedagogy	Andragogy
Self-concept	Dependency	Increasing self-directedness
Experience	Of little worth	Learners are a rich resource for learning
Readiness	Biological development Social pressure	Developmental tasks of social roles
Time Perspective	Postponed application	Immediacy of application
Orientation to learning	Subject centered	Problem centered

How do these assumptions relate to the trainee target? Frequently, because adults have not learned to be self-directing and have been dependent upon a teacher/trainer, they are uncomfortable and must be prepared to learn in this new way. Basic to this is a "psychologically safe" climate of trust, respect and acceptance. Being able to establish this safe learning climte is critical to all else that follows.

How do these assumptions relate to the organization? What kind of management philosophy does the organization employ, Theory X or Theory Y as described by McGregor?[4] These are basic assumptions about human behavior and human nature. Because of the emphasis on experiential learning in an andragogical approach, a Theory X organization would probably experience significant dissonance. Unless the training is intended to affect change in management philosophy, it probably would not be tolerated. Hence, support must be present or developed which will permit this kind of training design.

Knowles suggests that another critical question is how the organization views its long-range goals.[5] If the organization is changing and unstable, preparation of employees who are open to change and have a desire to learn and adapt is essential for the organization's long-range survival. Assumptions implicit in significant experiential learning as propounded by C. R. Rogers[6] and summarized by Knowles are as follows:

> Human beings have a natural potentiality for learning. Significant learning takes place when the subject matter is perceived by the student as relevant to his own purposes. Much significant learning is acquired through doing. Learning is facilitated by student's responsible participation in the learning process. Self-initiated learning involving the whole person--feelings as well as intellect--is the most pervasive and lasting. Creativity in learning is best facilitated when self-criticism and self-evaluation are primary, and evaluation by others is of secondary importance. The most socially useful thing to learning in the modern world is the process of learning, a continuing openness to experience, an incorporation into oneself of the process of change.[7]

If an organization cannot accept these notions about the adult learner, a training program built upon them is doomed to fail. If an organization wants employees trained so that only prescribed learning takes place, an approach designed to synergize the learning will not survive. The climate in the organization must make a positive statement that it cares about its employees and reinforce it by the way it develops its human resources.

Public Welfare, taken in the largest organizational sense, posesses many conflicts and problems for training and staff development. Interview training for the assistance payments function in today's welfare agency must reflect the goals of the agency, must be effective, and also must help the employee understand and cope with the forces operating on him. The organizational climate for which the trainer must prepare the assistance payments worker/interviewer is fraught with value conflict and stress. Unless the trainer prepares the employee for competent job performance which recognizes the influence of the organizational climate and agency goals, the trainer is setting up for failure both the employee and himself.

Today, there is a tremendous emphasis on measuring job performance in quantitative terms. "How much" has replaced "how well." It is critical to understand the influence of the organizational climate and value conflicts with which the trainer and trainee today must cope. Whence we came provides insight into where we are today and why and how we might evaluate the options open to us.

With the separation of the assistance payments and services functions in welfare in the 1970's, there came a departure in thrust and professional underpinning for the assistance payments function. Efficient, effective delivery of the money payment became the goal and error rate became the indicator for how successful states were in achieving this goal. Federal tolerance limits for errors were established, and states became caught up in activities related to error reduction.

The most powerful stimulus for such frenzy was the threat of federal fiscal sanction for errors over the tolerance levels. In the pursuit of ever greater accountability, states launched plans to reduce errors, increase productivity and improve effectiveness. Although this was certainly a stimulus for expansion of training programs, there have been many resultant organizational and educational issues with which training has had to deal.

Examples of such issues are: the emphasis on quantity vs. quality; paper-work vs. concern for people; high task orientation at the expense of job satisfaction vs. high task orientation paralleling high job satisfaction.

In the quest for efficiency and effectiveness, assistance payments left behind Social Work as a discipline and instead linked itself with public administration or management as its guiding knowledge and philosophy base, much the same as social work historically had linked itself with psychology and psychiatry. The linkage in many ways legitimized the new area or discipline. It reassured many administrators looking for solutions to tough problems that if you could define and quantify it, you could solve it. It provided measurement tools and concepts. It also brought with it norms and expectations that often conflicted with those already in existence--those that remained from the social work tradition. Social work was con-sidered soft because it resisted measurement and evaluation and dealt with intangibles like improving the quality of life. Management, on the other hand, is seen as tough because its capable of quantifying--a critical factor in demonstrations of success.

In the past and continuing today individuals enter the field of Public Welfare, be it services or assistance payments, with the idea that they are going to be helpful to those in need; that they are going to be dealing with people.

The reality for those in assistance payments is that the nature of the job has been redefined and is now heavily oriented toward information and data handling. Although an intake worker may be dealing with an individual under stress and/or in need, his job is frequently defined only in terms of obtaining accurate, reliable information, so that eligibility for a money payment can be determined without error. This reality is very different than the expectations. John Horejsi, Thomas Walz, and Patrick Connolly have discussed an extensive research project recently conducted in a public welfare agency in a large midwestern city. Of those individuals taking part in the study, these authors state:

> Roughly two-thirds (63 percent) traced their original commitment to the field of social welfare to a belief that it would allow them to act in a helping and supportive capacity and be of service to their community. Yet many workers found themselves caught up instead in clerical routines devoid of challenge, creativity, or direct human contact. Paper had somehow supplanted people.[8]

Even in direct client contact jobs that involve interviewing, the emphasis too frequently is on the paper transaction rather than the interpersonal interaction. Many employee problems like turnover, absenteeism and low morale can be traced to an individual's expectations that the job is going to be different than what is experienced. What the job has become has a great deal to do with the influence that has been exerted by management and business philosophy. In many segments of the welfare arena, workers discover that their performance is being measured only in quantitative terms, i.e., the number of intakes done per day, the number of paper transactions made, how long it takes to do a redetermination interview for eligibility purposes. The rub is around the expectation many hold when they accept a job in welfare that they are going to be making a difference in somebody's life, that they are in people-servicing work, and that how they conduct themselves is important.

An organization's health is dependent on the health of its members which is related to job satisfaction. Much job dissatisfaction can be traced to unfulfilled expectations about the intent of the job. If a program is to work, there must be clarity in its purpose and goals. Public Welfare is a value-laden area where there has never been real clarity.

Without real clarity as to what society wants welfare to be, workers become caught up in value conflicts and reflect this in how they do their jobs. If they work in direct client contact jobs as interviewers, the dilemma of who they are and how they are to relate is clearly conveyed. Society via the federal government has not really decided whether welfare should be an economic device, or a social control measure, or a client-oriented effort to improve the quality of life for the oppressed. Operationally, because there is no overriding purpose or direction overtly communicated, public welfare has fallen prey to the influence of fads and fantasies which seem to fill the void and supply the direction when it is not otherwise apparent.

Horejsi, et. al., define a fad as "any form of fashionable behavior that has been popularly accepted within some definable sociocultural milieu." A fantasy is "a mental image about the observable world which lacks a strong basis in reality." Management is normally a means to an end. However, the influence management has had suggests that in the absence of goal, purpose or direction, what normally is a means for goal achievement has moved in to fill the void that the absent goal should have supplied. The means then has become the end. All efforts have become directed toward perfecting the management of the system rather than improving the system through management techniques.[9] Horejsi, et. al., state,

> The Nixon Administration, encouraged in the early 1970's by the success of McNamara's application of "scientific management" to defense and space, began to introduce this style of management into other public sectors. Public Welfare was, of course, very susceptible to the fad and fantasy of "scientific management." The first step was to define the problems of the welfare system as a product of bad management. HEW then set out to design and introduce a new management and accountability system for welfare. Introduction of this philosophy was facilitated by the power of the purse and the federalization of the system's categorical assistance programs.

In this fashion, public welfare, in pursuit of greater management efficiency, became another computer-based industry re-programmed to fit the capacities of machine technology.

The fantasy, or course, was that the ills of welfare could be cured by improving management. The new victims of this delusion were the administrators and workers who could now be charged with administrative incompetency, or with too much foolhardy client advocacy.[10]

Hence, with the threat of federal fiscal sanction for errors and the promise that better management practices (as manifested by an emphasis on being able to quantify) might be the answer, the 1970's have represented an era of questionable accountability. Many workers believe that in a system presumably designed to service clients, accountability should be not only in terms of quantity but also in terms of quality--a much more difficult area to measure. Public Welfare workers are like other kinds of employees. Employees want to be competent and to be held accountable for a job well done. For what they are held accountable, however, is the significant question. What is taught in client contact training in areas like inter-viewing is even more significant.

Training and Staff Development's key mission is to provide properly trained staff for the agency's work. Without clarity of purpose out of which the work evolves, training of staff is very difficult. In pursuing an androgogical appraoch to training, one finds that he frequently assumes the role of consultant, with subroles of advocate, stimulator, and change agent. It is essential to help the organization clarify its problems and conflicts and the effects they produce.

One of the problems is the need for a reexamination of means and ends and a redefinition of philosophical base and a clarification of agency mission. Trying to legitimize the acceptance of a philosophical base which will not only hold people accountable for quantity, but also holds people accountable for quality is a critical task. This is a task that will be viable even as fads and fantasies come and go. Training must produce interviewers who can move papers to get the job done but it must also produce employees who competently, effectively and humanely do their jobs and obtain satisfaction in jobs well done.

Interviewing training can be a means or an end, a developmental process or a product. If you are a human resource development person trying to build toward a productive, supportive work environment, you may see it as both. Although the assistants payment job is data oriented, the value of respect for the individual remains as a residual from the social work tradition. Managerial effectiveness and efficiency and respect for individuals are not necessarily mutually exclusive. The two need not be in conflict. Staff development professionals must remember, however, that they are caught up in the accountability syndrome too, and must justify increasingly what they do in terms of a bottom line, not just in terms of personal or professional values.

Trainers must help the organization achieve its goals. This often means selling training to management in terms they understand. The best bottom line in the world is made by trainers who facilitate the development of employees who competently perform their client contacts efficiently, effectively, and humanely. To ground employees in what to ask and how to ask it, how to do their job, and how to help clients understand what they are to report, can have large payoffs in error reduction, avoidance of fraud cases, satisfaction that the client is getting everything he or she is entitled to, and knowledge that the system is working as it was designed. Good interviewing training can do this and in fact can have a synergistic effect. In essence, with good interviewing, concern for the client and effective, efficient delivery of the service will be communicated. One should not only learn skills during training but should also clarify his own attitudes about clients and welfare, explore potential job expectation conflicts, learn appropriate professional behaviors, and begin to fit into an agency support network that will affirm a positive, professional self concept--irrespective of whether he is a service worker or an assistance payment worker.

Unless training incorporates knowledge, behavior, skill and values, you will not have an effective worker. There must be congruity between the individual's value orientation, his role, the context of his client contact, and the individual's skill and knowledge. Only by integrating all of these kinds of learnings can an individual really be prepared to face effectively the job at hand.

What we try to do in our training programs is create a safe environment where trainees begin to see: (1) who they are; (2) what they bring to the job in the way of life experience; (3) how this influences what they will do on the job; (4) how they can try out new behaviors and skills based on the agency's expectations for job performance; and (5) how they can bring issues and potential conflict areas to the agency's attention.

Often, reality about the nature of the job is very difficult from the expectations a worker holds when he enters the system. Consequently, in any training for job competence, there needs to be a thorough examination of the new employee's perceptions and expectations of role as well as the detailed specification of the behavioral dimensions of the realities around the role.

This means that in training an assistance payment worker, it is necessary to provide structured experiences which will: (1) raise to his level of awareness his expectations as to what he will be doing on the job; (2) specify what the tasks really are; (3) compare the expectations to the reality; and (4) deal with either the congruency or the disparity during the training.

I suspect that much job turnover and worker burnout has to do with the conflict and frustration employees experience when they have not been thoroughly prepared or they have not thoroughly understood or accepted what they will be asked to do. The other aspect to this is related to prevailing attitudes on all levels that negatively reinforce the status of assistance payment worker--much the same as the status of client/recipient is negatively reinforced. Many assistance payment workers feel that it doesn't matter how well they do their jobs. Their jobs are devalued by society the way welfare recipients are devalued. They are defined as a necessary evils. People need and want to see themselves as doing worthwhile work, as competent. This is particularly true for individuals coming into public welfare because they want to help people in need.

If there is no positive reinforcement that the job of the assistance payment worker is worthwhile, it matters little that you've learned to do it extremely well. Training client contact persons in solid interviewing skills and behaviors that convey a positive professional self image and a positive acceptance of the client are the tasks. Helping management provide a supportive, healthy organizational climate that values life-long adult learning and growing is also the task. An andragogical approach to training can have large payoffs to the organization in increased morale, job satisfaction, and better skills however the total organization becomes the target. The mission becomes the creation of a supportive environment for employee and client alike which will remain adaptable and healthy irrespective of

change, fad or fantasy. An andragogical approach to training can be the
vehicle through which such a process can take place.

FOOTNOTES

1. Diane M. Simpson (Stagliano), <u>Interviewing Training Module</u> (Trenton: New Jersey Division of Public Welfare, Training and Staff Development Unit, 1975).

2. Malcolm Knowles, <u>The Adult Learner: A Neglected Species</u> (Houston: Gulf Publishings, 1973).

3. Ibid., p. 104.

4. D. McGregor, <u>The Human Side of Enterprise</u> (New York: McGraw-Hill, 1960), pp. 33-34 and 47-48.

5. Knowles, op. cit., pp. 94-97.

6. C. R. Rogers, <u>On Becoming a Person</u> (Boston: Houghton-Mifflin, 1961) pp. 272-279.

7. Knowles, op. cit., p. 95.

8. John Horejsi, Thomas Walz and Patrick Connolly, <u>Working in Welfare: Survival through Positive Action</u> (Iowa City: University of Iowa, School of Social Work, 1977) p. 16.

9. Ibid., p. 25.

10. Ibid., pp. 32-34.

Training and Gaming with Staff and Residents of a Half-Way House: or They All Train the Same, but Who Learns More?

by Judson H. Morris, Jr.

Judson H. Morris, Jr., M.S.W., is Clinic Director of the Umatilla County Mental Health Program in Umatilla, Oregon.

One of the many problems that state mental hospitals encounter is finding adequate half-way houses for their patients. Many of these houses are as far into the outer community as a half-way house resident will ever get, and this is especially true if the staff of the house is untrained in human services delivery.

One way to improve the existence of half-way house residents and facilitate their reentry into society is to train not only the staff but also the residents. Half-way house personnel should be trained together in one large training session, and staff and residents should be treated as equals. It has been said that in mental hospitals that the only way to distinguish staff from patients is that the staff have keys (symbols of power). In the case of an open half-way house, the staff and residents dress alike and, much of the time, they act the same. There are no keys, but there are more subtle forms of staff power. My objective in this training program was to discover if staff power could be shared and possibly redistributed, so that residents could begin to have the power and responsibility to manage their own lives, to make decisions, and, when the time was right, to move out of the half-way house and back into the community.

For four months I was a training consultant for a half-way house in
rural eastern Oregon. The staff of this half-way house consisted of four
family members and one training coordinator. Only the father had experience
in the mental health field (he had been a psychiatric technician aid for
six months, 20 years ago). The rest of the family had no prior human
services experience and were half-way house live-ins. The training coordinator,
who was responsible for resident activities, had a degree in elementary
education.

The 11 half-way house residents ranged in age from 25 to 75 years old.
There were eight females and three males. The residents had been hospitalized
on many occasions, and periods of commitment ranged from six months to 50
years. Some of these hospitalizations were at the state hospital and
others were at various residential care facilities.

The training program consisted of training in a method of intervention
or communication. This was followed by a problem case presentation, using
the method learned to solve that particular problem. Handouts and other
materials were also used in the training. The training program was conducted
for two hours every week for four months, and consisted of:

- Training Needs Assessment

- Resident Profile

- Problem Solving Model

- Community Meetings

- Behavior Modification

- Performance Contracting

- Token Economics

- Crisis Intervention Techniques

- Review

- Positive Strokes Game

- The Newspaper Game

- Give n' Take

- Three Easy Squares

- Hollow Square Exercise

- Spin n' Solve

- Training Evaluations

The training sessions were sequenced, beginning with very elementary communication and problem solving training devices, and progressing to more difficult problem solving and communication exercises. Many of these training simulations involved appropriate confrontation, task operationalizing, and problem solving through shared decision making.

After I had first trained the staff in various intervention modalities, I began to involve the residents in the training. This sequence of staff development and training gave the staff feelings of competence and confidence, diminished their feelings of being threatened and made them less defensive when the residents were invited to participate in the last half of the training. In fact, the staff thought that involving the residents in training was a great idea.

The residents and staff stated that their problems at the house centered around communication. The residents also related to the trainer that many of their problems in the community (before their hospitalizations) were in communication (what they told people they were thinking and how). On the basis of this information, the focus of training was changed from improving the staff's intervention skills to improving intervention and communication skills for the staff and residents. Simulations were used, and all members

of the house were given roles to solve the assigned task and to improve
their decision making and communication. For training purposes, the simulations almost completely integrated the staff and residents: they were all
treated alike, and they began to treat each other as equals. This spilled
over beyond the training sessions into the way that the staff interacted
with themselves and the residents, and into the way that the residents
interacted with each other. Effective training has carry-over beyond the
training situation, and this occurred. In the simulations, the staff and
residents were dependent upon each other to solve problems. They were able
to see that the very survival of the half-way house and of its personnel
depended on cooperation. The residents started to solve their own problems
with each other and the staff through the use of the daily community meetings,
or through an individual problem solving group encounter. Because of this,
both residents and staff felt more comfortable in allowing the residents to
begin to venture out beyond the half-way house and to acquire part-time
jobs in the community.

The house residents performed better in the problem solving and communication training simulations than did the staff, because they were more task
oriented and not as easily distracted. My explanation of this phenomenon,
the "tortoise and hare theory," is contrary to the notion that persons of
lower intelligence can handle simple monotonous tasks better than "normal"
persons because they are not as easily distracted. The staff discounted
the intelligence of the residents and how quickly and accurately they could
accomplish a complicated task. At times the staff "sloughed off" the
training assignment until too late. The residents performed better when
they were expected by the trainer to perform on the same level or better

than everyone else, including the staff. Many of the residents had institutionalized intelligence and behaviors; they were expected to act "retarded" and "developmentally disabled," and they complied. Now the residents were expected to complete complicated tasks, and they did! The residents completed the tasks as fast, if not faster, than high school students and on one occasion, they completed a complicated planning-task training simulation faster than human services professionals.

For me, the half-way house training was very exciting and meaningful. The training of the staff began to reach its limits and I began to run out of training ideas. Once I involved the residents, however, the training horizons opened up. I was able to find material from management, communications, problem solving and many other areas of training, and all the house personnel enjoyed the training.

At the end of the training sequence, all participants evaluated the training. This was done anonymously and face-to-face. All participants stated that they had learned a great deal. It was my observation that though the staff might have learned as much as the residents, the residents had come further from the behavioral and communication deficits that they had prior to training. The residents were now solving their own problems and making decisions governing their own lives, rather than being the passive dependents of the half-way house staff. In the evaluation sessions, all the house personnel identified positive behavioral changes among the residents and their interactions with other residents and staff and a skill change in the way the staff interacted with each other and the residents.

Peer approval and approval from others was reinforcing to the residents, as it is to any individual. Because they had not been treated so during previous hospitalizations, the residents of the half-way house responded positively to being treated as equals, especially by a human services person (the trainer). The half-way house residents responded more openly when their opinions and their ideas were valued by the other residents and a human services person from the community and especially by the half-way house staff. If all these people could accept what they were saying and accept them as people, maybe others in the outer community could also.

So began the process of developing alternative living situations and employment arrangements for the residents of the half-way house. Success in the management of their own lives, the ability to set and obtain goals, and freedom of choice were the areas in which residents and staff wanted improvement. The staff felt more confident and competent, started to view the residents as being more competent and began to delegate more personal power and decision making to the residents. As a result, the residents began to manage their own lives, much to everyone's approval.

Most of the time, people can perform according to the expectation of achieving agreed-upon goals. By setting obtainable goals, there developed a self-fulfilling prophecy for success and the expectations of increasing skills, competence, confidence, and self-worth were met.

Action and Reaction

One of the stated purposes of the training program at the half-way house was to improve communication between staff and residents and to increase the residents' responsibility in governing their own lives. Once the training had concluded, the residents were more ready to assume some of the responsibilities in running the group home than were the staff. These responsibilities were not to involve financial and legal matters (everyone agreed these tasks should remain the function of the staff), but would include some of the program decisions and day-to-day operations of the half-way house. The residents were ready to provide input and accept some delegated responsibilities and assignments.

However, when the residents of the half-way house wanted to get involved in running the house, there was reactionary behavior on the part of the staff. Except for the educational trainer, the staff was ready to leave things as they were, with the exception that residents could be made more responsible for household chores and keeping their rooms clean. The staff did not want to delegate any of the responsibility for running the half-way house to the residents because of a fear of loss of power. This was the case even when a resident was as qualified if not more so for a job assignment than a staff member (one of the residents was a head cook at the local state hospital and even she was not allowed to be involved with meal planning and preparation for the half-way house). This situation caused the residents much frustration and they began to lapse into "institutional" silence to avoid contact and confrontations with the staff.

After the initial impact of the extensive communications and problem solving training that the staff and residents shared and changes that followed in the running of the half-way house, conditions in the house returned to where they were before the training. A "rubber band" effect had occurred; the opportunities for shared staff and resident responsibility had initially expanded, but now had contracted.

After being involved with the first four months of training and change and then viewing the next three months of reentrenchment, the question I now ask myself is: Was the training worth it, especially in light of the feelings of initial success by the residents, which were later replaced by frustrations? What could have been done to create a balance, so that some middle position where both the staff and the residents shared more responsibilities was possible. Was it better to have left the residents and the staff of the half-way house alone and never tried the training? I doubt it. One thing that is now apparent to me is that the training must be ongoing and continually self-monitoring, at least at this half-way house. As one of the adult children of the house's head staff member informed me, "My father just feels threatened by the fear of a loss of power and the eroding of his power base."

FOOTNOTES

1. Fred Cox, et. al., <u>Strategies of Community Organization</u> (Itasca, Illinois: F. E. Peacock Publishers, Inc., 1974), pp. 425-444.

2. Judson H. Morris, Jr., and Lynne Clemmons Morris, "Workshop On Performance Contracting in The Human Services" (Pasco, Washington: 1976).

3. Judson H. Morris, Jr., Lynne Clemmons Morris and Erving Ruhl, "When The Chips Are Down--A Game Video-Social Simulation Training Device," State of Oregon, Mental Health Division, 1978.

4. Michael Giametteo, "The Positive Strokes Game" (Vancouver, Washington: Sylvan Institute, 1977).

5. Stephen Curtin and John Washburn, "The Newspaper Game," <u>Simulation/Gaming</u>, Vol. 1, No. 4 (January 1973), p. 15.

6. Don Ifill, "Give n' Take," <u>Simulation Therapy Conference, Journal of Conference Proceedings</u> (University of California, Riverside, Simulation Therapy Institute, 1974), pp. 31-35.

7. J. William Pfeiffer and John E. Jones, <u>A Handbook Of Structured Experience For Human Relations Training</u>, Volume II (LaJolla, California: University Associate Publishers, Inc., 1970), pp. 32-40.

8. Judson H. Morris, Jr., "Spin n' Solve--A Game Of Shared Decision Making of Alternative Strategies in An Environment with Conflicting Populations," <u>International Simulation and Gaming Association Annual Conference, Journal of Conference Proceedings</u> (Berlin, West Germany: Technische Universitat Berlin, 1974).

Training Nursing Home Administrators Concerning the Role and Value of Social Services

by Gemma Beckley and Gary Mooers

Gemma Beckley, M.S.W., is Assistant Professor of Social Work at the University of Mississippi. Gary R. Mooers, Ph.D., is Director of the University of Mississippi Social Work Program.

Introduction

One of the most significant recent developments in medical social work has been the growth of social services in nursing homes and extended care centers. Although this development may be due, in part, to an increased appreciation of the values of social services in such settings, it is primarily attributable to both federal and state regulations which mandate these services for both successful licensure and reimbursement for patient care. These regulations have met with somewhat less than universal acclaim from administrators of these facilities who often see mandatory social services (and the required treatment plans and other related paperwork) as just another burden imposed by various layers of governmental bureaucracy. This feeling on the part of administrators is exacerbated by the fact that many of them have only the vaguest notion of what social services are or what they are intended to accomplish.

Consequently, a series of regional workshops for nursing home administrators were devised by the Social Work Program and the Division of Special Activities at the University of Mississippi. These seminars were approved

for licensure credit by the Mississippi State Board of Nursing Home Administrators, which made attendance more attractive for the participants.

The basic purpose for these workshops was to acquaint nursing home
administrators with the profession of social work and to show the value of
social services within the nursing home setting. We were acutely aware of
the fact that we were promoting services that cost money and do not bring
in additional revenue to a group of practical cost-conscious administrators.
Because of the nature of the audience, the format of the presentations
emphasized practicality and stressed the tangible benefits which could
result from effective social service delivery.

The workshops, which were a day and a half in length, were broken down
into five sessions, each of which had a distinct function. The first
session focused on the profession of social work because of the belief that
the participants would need this background if they were to understand the
role of social services in their own specialized area. The second session
also avoided the specific area of social services and was concerned with
the social and emotional needs of nursing home patients. The final three
sessions dealt with social services in nursing home facilities and consisted
of discussions of the role and functions of social workers in such facilities,
priority setting, and typical problems which arise in nursing home social
service delivery.

Social Work Profession

Presenting a broad overview of the profession of social work entails a
familiar dilemma to those who provide training for other professions and
disciplines. How does one interpret the many facets of this profession to
an audience which may view social work as being strictly confined to welfare

programs for the poor or see it as a process engaged in by wealthy matrons to ease the plight of the less fortunate.

The approach utilized in this situation may prove helpful to others who find it necessary to explain (and possibly defend) the profession of social work. This paper began with a definition stressing trained personnel, problem solving and problems in social functioning. In other words, education, the helping process and primary target groups were all covered. As with all definitions, the definition was tailored to the specific group or audience.

After a brief discussion of the decline of primary group relationships in this society, we elaborated on the need for the helping professions to fill roles previously handled by the family, the church and the neighborhood or village structure. The profession of social work as a profession was then covered extensively in terms of what makes up a profession and how social work successfully meets this criteria. This was followed by a brief treatment of the recent expansion of the profession, its number of practitioners, and the number of educational institutions now offering professional education in social work. Finally, projections for further growth were presented and examined.

One issue which must inevitably be treated is that social workers are not universally loved and respected. This fact was acknowledged and then interpreted as being logical for the profession (more than any other) which has chosen to work with the "hurts and ills" of this society. The unpopularity of certain client groups (e.g., the welfare poor) has reflected negatively upon those professionals involved in trying to alleviate and eradicate the problems of these client groups.

In an era of competing professions and blurred professional boundaries, the unique expertise of social work must be identified and expounded to groups such as nursing home administrators. Social work, with its emphasis on man as a social being and its knowledge that problems involve persons in social situations, is uniquely suited to help people with many of the problems that arise in modern society. Concrete examples were given involving nursing home patients who are not merely patients but persons with social networks both inside and outside the facility. Breakdowns in social functioning as well as essentially personal problems may require the assistance of a trained social worker.

The final segment in this introductory session involved the knowledge, values and skills of the social work profession. The educational process was described and each broad educational component was examined. The value system of social work was also covered with its emphasis on human dignity and self-determination. Finally, social work skills were discussed in terms of interviewing skills, diagnosis, observation, and recording and writing skills.

This entire session was aimed at providing the audience with a beginning knowledge of what social work was, the areas in which it functioned, the expertise it has demonstrated, and the knowledge, values and skills which embody this profession. After this information was imparted, it was then deemed appropriate to examine closely the social and emotional needs of nursing home patients and their families.

Needs of Nursing Home Patients and Their Families

The content of this session was devised to emphasize to administrators that competent medical care, sanitary physical conditions and nutritious meals are not enough to ensure successful patient care. It focused on social work functions and tasks throughout the client's contact with the facility from preadmission to discharge. Emphasis was placed on how effective social services could benefit the client, his family and the nursing home itself.

Philosophically the right to self-determination is an important consideration to potential nursing home clients and their families. People prefer to remain in the familiar surroundings of their homes in the later years when so many familiar things have slipped away. In considering this basic philosophy, every effort should be made and every community resource explored before institutionalization is considered. Unless the client prefers an extended care facility it should be a last resort, because the experience is often traumatic even when every effort is made to overcome the inevitable feelings of abandonment and rejection.

Individual differences play an important part in determining the best care plan for the older person experiencing problems in functioning. Balancing respect for the needs, attitudes and right of self-determination of the elderly and the desire of family and professionals to provide care and protection is difficult to say the least. Assessing the client's strengths, weaknesses and assets, rather than concentrating on deficiencies, appears to be one of the first steps. A good treatment plan will be based on this assessment and should create a realistic awareness within the client and family to assist them in making appropriate decisions. This stage of planning is crucial in setting the tone or atmosphere for future considerations and efforts with the clients and their families. If at all possible, everyone must be included at this stage to encourage a realistic decision.

Each step in the phases of assistance before admission, during admission and upon discharge has its individual importance in the role of the social worker as a helper. Frequently the professional can make the difference in lessening the degree of trauma that will be experienced by clients and their families.

The decision to apply for nursing home admission is the very first step in which the social worker can offer assistance. The feelings of alienation and abandonment can be dealt with at this time. The family often feels guilty for suggesting the application because of strong belief that the elderly are the family's responsibility and because the elderly person often does not want to leave home. The patient, even with the highest level of intelligence and understanding, tends to experience fear and anxiety. Common concerns at this time are fear of the unknown, worries of regimentation, and the image of nursing homes as places where people go to die. Acknowledge these feelings of abandonment, guilt and fear and then move to the reality based determinants of the placement. The necessity of everyone's participation at this stage becomes more crucial than ever, even with the most impaired clients.

Once the application has been completed, a second important phase of assistance is the waiting period. Even after making the decision that an extended care facility is the most practical and realistic route for the patient, many feelings of concern and anxiety are prevalent during the waiting period. There is almost always a waiting period between application and admission. An occasional telephone call or possibly a visit from the social worker helps to reassure the people involved and to develop a good relationship between family and the facility. This serves as an aid in avoiding some of the relocation trauma that frequently occurs in the next phase of the admission process.

The third phase of assistance is admission. Statistics reviewed indicate that transplantation shock apparently takes it toll on many clients. The death rate during the early days of nursing home residence is sufficiently high to indicate that necessary planning is often neglected in admission to these facilities. It appears that newly admitted clients are often not prepared psychologically for the move and are not emotionally equipped to cope with the stresses of new environmental surroundings.

During the client's residency every effort should be made to encourage maintenance of reality contact and opportunities for personal fulfillment should be provided in as many ways as possible. The social worker can serve effectively as a liaison between family, institution and patient.

A final phase of assistance comes at the time of death or discharge. The focus of the professional is either utilization of a resource more in keeping with the client's goals or consolation to the family if the family member dies. Community image of the nursing home can be improved greatly during this phase. A staff member, preferably the social worker or administrator, should visit the family at the time of bereavement. This visit can help the family work through the grief process and emphasize that the client was regarded as a respected and valued person by the nursing home staff.

The Social Worker in the Nursing Home Setting

The third session reinforced some major points presented in the preceding session and attempted to separate and differentiate social services in nursing home settings from other areas of practice. A major goal in this session was to bring into focus the specific tasks social workers needed to perform in order to enrich and simplify the lives of nursing home clients.

This session began with a ten minute film from Yugoslovia entitled "Weekend," which portrays the abandonment of an old man by his family and implies that abandonment and rejection are the fate of the elderly in modern societies. This excellent film invariably left the audience divided into two groups: those who were utterly bewildered by the film's subtle message and those who quickly perceived the global implications of what this film had to say. This always led into discussions concerning the problems that elderly persons and their families ultimately face.

The nursing home setting was discussed in terms of the fact that it is one of the more difficult settings in which to practice and it requires specialized skills. Two specific essentials for the social worker in the nursing home setting were stressed. They were maintaining optimism in an often unoptimistic setting and effectively communicating with individuals who often have physical or mental impairments interfering with communication.

The basic social work skills were again emphasized (interviewing, observation, relationship building, diagnosis and recording) and were placed in perspective. All of these skills need to be developed and sharpened when working with individuals facing typical problems of the institutionalized aged such as terminal conditions, chronic illness, alienation and depression.

Specific tasks of the nursing home social worker were covered in some detail so the administrators could begin to get a feel for just what the social worker should be doing. As with any list of tasks, these were an arbitrary number chosen to illustrate both the seriousness and the diversity of this area of practice. These tasks involved recording of these contacts and contacts with the client, the client's family and the community. The previously mentioned skills were blended with the tasks so the participants could identify certain skills which needed to be utilized in performing certain tasks.

The session ended with a discussion focusing on how much the well-being of the clients would be enhanced and how much everyone's job would be made easier and more pleasurable if the nursing home social worker skillfully performed the tasks mentioned in this session. The social worker's function was interpreted as being as important as that of the registered nurse, pharmacist or dietitian.

Setting Priorities in Nursing Homes

What are the most apparent and pressing needs for the utilization of social work personnel in a nursing home setting? When all of the needs that were outlined in this workshop are considered, it is logical that administrators will begin to feel overwhelmed. In this session, most of the essentials for acceptable social work practice were specified. This particular part of the workshop was aimed at identifying the most important social work functions which must be carried out if effective care is to be given to residents.

There are obvious limitations on how much work can be done by staff in nursing homes. There is simply not sufficient money to hire enough staff to make a profit and fulfill every discipline's suggestion of essentials or preferred treatment. In view of this situation, what are the most obvious needs for the utilization of social work staff in a nursing home? In a nursing home with a capacity of 60 patients, at least one BSW should be employed to provide the social service functions and to work as a team member with other professionals to ensure total patient care. The social workers' responsibility should include the following.

1. They should be responsible for admission, including interpreting the regulations of the nursing home, rendering support, helping

families make appropriate decisions, and evaluating the needs of clients entering the facility.

2. Upon admission, they should secure all essential background information from agencies that will aid in the support of the client and in determining what can be done with and for a client. It is important to obtain as clear a background of the client as possible, and such information can either be obtained through family or agencies that might be familiar with the client. Besides developing relationships with other agencies that can serve as appropriate referral or needed backup for those services that cannot be offered in the nursing home, it aids in the nursing home's ability to assist in the client's adjustment.

3. In conjunction with other staff, they should bring a perspective to planning for a client that is brought only by this profession.

4. They should carry out goals for the patient, with other staff, on a daily therapeutic basis such as in reality orientation or supportive therapy.

5. They should keep required records such as those for medicaid commissions and state boards of health, if client progress is to be examined. Constantly updated goals with goal-oriented progress notes helps keep the staff on track and addresses the client's individual needs. Constant assessment is needed to ensure that relevant goals are being pursued and that the methods to reach these goals are realistic and consistent. Another part of record keeping is a narrative history which should be a thorough history of the client's past. Any information that will help one to understand the client's behavior and give a guide to what can be

expected in terms of adjustment is helpful. A review of adjust-
ments to other situations (e.g., previous hospitalizations)
serves as a clue to what may prove successful in the client's
adjustment to the nursing home. A continuing plan of care should
include consideration of a transfer to more desirable living
conditions.

6. They should provide assistance when death comes, since the way
    that this is handled affects attitudes toward nursing homes for
    generations to come. The family may need a social worker and
    someone should be available to show that the institution cares.
    The effort and concern of a trained social worker at this time
    can be invaluable to family members.

Common Problems in Nursing Home Social Work

The final session was concerned with typical problems that occur in
nursing home situations. After a brief discussion of the universality and
inevitability of problems, five hypothetical problems involving nursing
home patients and personnel were presented to the participants for discussion.
The final session was designed in this manner because it seemed to the
instructors that the participants had probably reached the saturation point
in terms of being able to absorb new knowledge.

The five problems involved:

1. The withdrawn, depressed and deteriorating new patient.

2. The disagreeable and obstreperous patient who refuses to cooperate
    with staff, family or medical personnel.

3. The well-meaning family that endangers the patient's health with
    overly long visits and supplies of forbidden food (sweets for the
    diabetics).

-221-

4. The patient who has "retired" to the wheelchair even though there is no physical ailment which precludes walking.

5. A conflict situation between the social worker and the nurse over appropriate role definitions.

These discussions were well received and the participants went beyong the exmaples to bring up current problems in their own facilities. The instructors guided these discussions, pointing out on several occasions how a trained social worker could be effectively utilized in resolving or improving certain problem areas.

Evaluation of the Workshop

As with any undertaking, success is measured by what one hoped to accomplish. It would be nice to be able to say that all of the participants were instantly converted to the idea of a strong service program and left the workshop fully intending to hire the most qualified social worker available. Of course, this did not happen nor did we expect such a conversion to occur.

Certain positive aspects about the series of workshops certainly come to mind. The participants found the workshops to be entertaining and interesting. The level of interest among participants was consistently high an evidenced by the thoughtful questions which were asked in response to presented material. The workshops introduced the participants to the profession of social work and they left with a much clearer perspective about social services in the nursing home setting.

How much of this knowledge will be translated into positive steps to implement effective social service programs is a matter of conjecture. But the material was positively received and if the participants came out of the sessions viewing social services as an asset rather than a burdensome governmental requirement, then the workshops achieved their primary objective.